Being Novice School Teachers in China

PETER LANG
PROMPT

Qiqiang Xie and Yulong Li

Being Novice School Teachers in China

Concerns and Development in Knowledge, Skills, and Ethics

PETER LANG
Lausanne • Berlin • Bruxelles • Chennai • New York • Oxford

Library of Congress Cataloging-in-Publication Data

Names: Xie, Qiqiang, 1992– author. | Li, Yulong, 1988– author.
Title: Being novice school teachers in China : concerns and development in knowledge, skills, and ethics / Qiqiang Xie and Yulong Li.
Description: New York : Peter Lang, 2023. | Includes bibliographical references.
Identifiers: LCCN 2023008591 (print) | LCCN 2023008592 (ebook) | ISBN 9781433194351 (hardback) | ISBN 9781433196379 (ebook) | ISBN 9781636673028 (epub)
Subjects: LCSH: First-year teachers—China. | Teachers—In-service training—China. | Teachers—Professional ethics—China.
Classification: LCC LB2844.1.N4 X54 2023 (print) | LCC LB2844.1.N4 (ebook) | DDC 371.1020951—dc23/eng/20230313
LC record available at https://lccn.loc.gov/2023008591
LC ebook record available at https://lccn.loc.gov/2023008592
DOI 10.3726/b19599

Bibliographic information published by the **Deutsche Nationalbibliothek**.
The German National Library lists this publication in the German National Bibliography; detailed bibliographic data is available on the Internet at http://dnb.d-nb.de.

Cover design by Peter Lang Group AG

ISBN 9781433194351 (hardback)
ISBN 9781433196379 (ebook pdf)
ISBN 9781636673028 (epub)
DOI 10.3726/b19599

© 2023 Qiqiang Xie and Yulong Li
Published by Peter Lang Publishing Inc., New York, USA
info@peterlang.com - www.peterlang.com

All rights reserved.
All parts of this publication are protected by copyright.
Any utilization outside the strict limits of the copyright law, without the permission of the publisher, is forbidden and liable to prosecution.
This applies in particular to reproductions, translations, microfilming, and storage and processing in electronic retrieval systems.

This publication has been peer reviewed.

Table of Contents

List of Figures ix
List of Tables xi
Acknowledgements xiii
List of Abbreviations xv

Chapter One: Introduction 1
    1.1 Background 1
    1.2 Purpose of the Study 3
    1.3 Research Questions 4
    1.4 Significance of the Study 4
    1.5 Structure 5
Chapter Two: Literature Review 7
    2.1 The New Curriculum Reform in China 7
        2.1.1 Impact of the New Curriculum Reform 8
        2.1.2 Requirements of the Reform for Teachers 8
    2.2 Teacher Professional Development 9
        2.2.1 Definition of Teacher Professional Development 9
        2.2.2 Developmental Stages of TPD 11
        2.2.3 Characteristics of Novice Teachers' Development 13
    2.3 Implementation of Teacher Professional Development 17

TABLE OF CONTENTS

    2.3.1 Studies on Efficient Implementations of Teacher Professional Development 17
    2.3.2 Policy Support for the Implementation of TPD in China 19
    2.3.3 Deficiencies in the Implementation under the Reform in China 20
  2.4 Summary 21
Chapter Three: Methodology 23
  3.1 The Nature of Qualitative Research Approaches 23
  3.2 Methods of Data Collection 25
    3.2.1 Interviews 25
    3.2.2 Interview Questions 26
    3.2.3 Interview Procedure 28
  3.3 Sampling 28
  3.4 Data Analysis 30
  3.5 Limitations of the Study 32
Chapter Four: Findings and Analysis 33
  4.1 Background of the Interviewees 33
  4.2 Perception of Qualities of Professional Teacher 36
  4.3 Challenges for Novice Teachers 39
    4.3.1 Challenges in Professional Ethics 39
    4.3.2 Challenges in Professional Skills 40
    4.3.3 Challenges in Professional Knowledge 44
    4.3.4 Negative Outcomes of the Challenges 45
  4.4 Current Opportunities for TPD of Novice Teachers 46
    4.4.1 School Programs of Promoting TPD for Novice Teachers 47
    4.4.2 Individual Strategies for Promoting TPD 49
    4.4.3 State Programs of Promoting TPD for Novice Teachers 51
  4.5 Current Needs and Expectations 53
    4.5.1 Expected Support from the State 53
    4.5.2 Expected Support from the School 54
    4.5.3 Personal Goals for Future Development 55
Chapter Five: Discussions and Conclusions 57
  5.1 Summary of Findings 57
    5.1.1 Teacher Professional Competence 59
    5.1.2 Challenges and Negative Outcomes 60
    5.1.3 Development Opportunities 61
    5.1.4 Needs and Expectation 63
    5.1.5 Differences between Rural and Urban Areas 63

	5.2	Implications	64
	5.3	Conclusion	65

References 67

List of Figures

Figure 3.1	Intercepted fragment of coding 1&2	31
Figure 4.1	Professional competencies of teachers	38
Figure 4.2	Challenges for novice teachers	45
Figure 4.3	Current opportunities in teacher professional development	53
Figure 5.1	Framework of teacher professional competence	60
Figure 5.2	Teacher professional development programs and strategies	62

List of Tables

Table 3.1   Information of the interviewees   29
Table 5.1   A synthesis of multi-level analysis of findings   58

Acknowledgements

We would like to express our heartfelt thanks to Dr. Qian Haiyan and Dr. Ko Yue On James, who offered the lead author tremendous support and valuable comments on the original version of the manuscript, which was finally developed into the current book as a result of our joint effort. Furthermore, we would also like to appreciate the professional service provided by Farideh Koohi-Kamali and Suma George from PETER LANG. The publishing of the study is supported by Macao Foundation (NO.MF2107).

List of Abbreviations

EdB   Education Bureau
MoE   Ministry of Education
TPD   Teacher Professional Development
UNESCO   United Nations Educational, Scientific and Cultural Organization

CHAPTER ONE

Introduction

Novice teachers are in a crucial period where they need to integrate theory with practice. Opportunities for teacher professional development (TPD) can help them overcome difficulties and improve their situations. In this regard, this research attempts to explore novice teachers' current opportunities and needs for professional development.

This chapter briefly introduces the background of the study. It starts with the requirements and expectations for teachers and then is followed by the importance of professional development for novice teachers and the purpose and questions that guide the study. After stating the significance, this chapter ends with the structure of this book.

1.1 Background

In a knowledge society, everyone should know about advanced ideas and information technology, and make preparations for lifelong learning and good social communication and collaboration skills (Dumont, Istance, & Benavides, 2010). That is the requirement for education, just as United Nations Educational, Scientific and Cultural Organization points out, we must cultivate our later generations to have the required capacities to face the crucial problems of the world and meet the challenge of future society (UNESCO, 2012). Therefore, to guarantee such education that could adapt the future development, we need "new" teachers. With the expectations of society rising, the teachers' role is becoming more and more complicated and demanding. The main task of teachers is not only transmitting knowledge but also organizing an environment for individuals to learn in their knowledge acquisition (Zuljan & Požarnik, 2014).

All the educational reforms in the world are aiming to enhance school effectiveness, and teachers are the crucial factors for success (Chow, 2016). Meanwhile, all the teachers and teaching are also influenced by the reforms (Chen & Day, 2015). In mainland China, since the launch of the curriculum reform in 2001, it has put forward higher requirements for teachers. The new curriculum standard emphasizes improving students' humane and scientific accomplishment, cultivating them to have the innovation spirit, the consciousness of cooperation, and a broader vision, together with basic abilities, such as reading comprehension, expression, and collaboration, as well as using modern technology to collect and process information (Ministry of Education, 2002). The reforms called for teachers to develop new competence and capacities (Qian & Walker, 2013).

However, for novice teachers, as their teaching experience are less than three years and their teaching tends to focus on survival (Huberman, Grounauer, Marti, & Neufeld, 1993), it is difficult to reach such high requirements. Moreover, due to a lack of enough teaching experience, many novice teachers often face challenges, such as managing the order of classrooms, using the proper technology, adopting effective teaching pedagogy, and handling community relationship (Kumi-Yeboah & James, 2012), which may depress novice teachers and influence the whole teaching accomplishment (Fantilli & McDougall, 2009).

The such issue should be highly emphasized. As novice teachers are a new force and an important part of the teaching teams, the stage they occupy is an indispensable and crucial period that integrates theory with practice. Although many of them learned the pragmatic facets of professional practice when they were student teachers, it only developed their competence in classroom teaching, not professional competence (Tang, Wong & Cheng, 2016). Most of the experiences that combine theory with the practice of teachers are from their novice period. This period will not only determine whether the novice teachers will continue to work in the field of teaching, but also decide what kind of teachers they will be (Xu, 2013). Therefore, it is very significant to deem highly of teacher professional development of novice teachers. Effective professional development can not only largely enhance the subject and pedagogical knowledge of teachers (Kumi-Yeboah & James, 2012), but also help novice teachers avoid negative outcomes (Gordon, 2004).

In the last three decades, there some researchers who studied in the field of teacher professional development of novice teachers had put forward a lot of concepts and models in teacher training and teacher development. For instance, there are some concepts based on the *"professional development/learning community"* (Hadar & Brody, 2010; 2013; Servage, 2009) or *"school-based training"* (Vonk, 1995; Lindgren, 2005) that aim at teachers' professional development, as well as some models and systems developed from the ideas such as *"teacher professional development school"* (Darling-Hammond, 1994; Avalos, 2011), *"mentoring system"* (Huling & Resta, 2001; Kajs, 2002; Blair, 2008). These research results have made a significant contribution to promoting novice teachers' professional development. However, compared with these studies from developed countries, research on teacher professional development in China started much later. In 2002, the Ministry of Education of China firstly proposed the concept of *"teacher professional development"*, with the issue of the policy document *Ministry of Education's Suggestions on Reform and Development of Teacher Education During the Period of "Tenth Five Year-Plan"* (Ministry of Education, 2002). After that, some relevant policies have been being introduced in successions, such as the *National Mid-term and Long-term Education Reform and Development Program Outline (2010& 2012)* (Ministry of Education, 2010), *Ministry of Education's Suggestions on Strengthening Teachers' Training in Primary and Middle Schools* (Ministry of Education, 2011), and *State Council's Suggestions on Strengthening the Construction of Teaching Team* (State Council, 2012). With the introduction of these policies, more and more researchers began to explore effective strategies for teacher professional development. However, according to the existing research results and data, many of the researchers in the field of TPD tend to focus on experienced or expert teachers, or even preservice teachers, while the researches aiming at novice teachers' professional development are correspondingly limited.

1.2 Purpose of the Study

This study attempts to investigate the current situations and characteristics of novice teachers' professional development in primary schools in mainland China through interviews. The study probes novice teachers' perception of teacher professional development, as well as the challenges and development opportunities they meet. Their current needs and expectations are also a focus of the investigation. Based on the theoretical framework, this study explores and summarizes the appropriate countermeasure and effective strategies for novice teachers to promote and improve their development.

1.3 Research Questions

Based on the purposes mentioned above, this study focus on the situation of novice teachers' professional development in primary schools. As the success of a novice teacher is determined by whether she or he perseveres in their quest to become a successful teacher (Kumi-Yeboah & James, 2012), the first research question is set to probe whether they have a will to improve themselves, and what professional competences they want to develop. In order to grasp the current contents and features of novice teachers' professional development, the next two questions are respectively set to find out what challenges and difficulties they met, and whether these difficulties exerted a negative influence on them, as well as examine the current strategies and programs of promoting their professional development. Additionally, the last question focus on their needs and expectations, probing the existing deficiencies of the implementation of teacher professional development. The specific research questions are listed as follows:

- Q1: What are the novice teachers' perceptions of teacher professional competence?
- Q2: What challenges and difficulties have the novice teachers met? And how do these difficulties influence them?
- Q3: What programs and strategies are adopted to promote novice teachers' professional development?
- Q4: What are the needs and expectations of novice teachers for continuous teacher professional development?

1.4 Significance of the Study

Novice teachers are in the early years of their careers, which is a crucial and potentially difficult period that will exert a far-reaching influence on their future (Öztürk, 2008; Paula & Grīnfelde, 2018). This study hopes to provide theoretical support and convincing empirical materials that may help novice teachers improve their professional development, enhance their teaching effectiveness, and enrich the theories of the field of teacher professional development. In addition, it can provide a reference not only for the school leaders or governments to make decisions or policies but also for the educators to effectively carry out school-based research.

1.5 Structure

This book is organized into five chapters. Chapter One is an introduction to the study, including the research questions and its background, as well as the purpose and significance of the study. Chapter Two provides conceptual context by examining selected literature on teacher professional development and the new curriculum reform. It covers the perception of teacher professional development, the characteristics of TPD of novice teachers, the requirements for TPD of the new curriculum reform, and the implementations of TPD. Chapter Three sets out the research methodology and methods, and provides a detailed description of the research process and the approach to the data analysis. Chapter Four contains the main findings of the study. It begins with the novice teachers' perception of professional competence and the dominant challenges and difficulties of them, followed by the current opportunities and expectations for teacher professional development of novice teachers. These findings are further discussed in the last chapter. In light of the literature reviewed in Chapter Two, Chapter Five draws a conclusion with a discussion about the current content and feature of the teacher professional development of novice teachers, and then draws the implications of the study, and a brief statement of the limitations.

CHAPTER TWO

Literature Review

The theoretical foundation and rationale of the research are provided by the review of the literature. This chapter explores the context of the new curriculum reform within which novice teachers start their teaching career and also reviews theories and studies on teacher professional development. Specifically, the reviewed literature mainly includes the impact of the new curriculum reform on teachers, the concepts of teacher professional development and novice teacher, and the theories and practices of the implementation of teacher professional development.

2.1 The New Curriculum Reform in China

Since the early 1980s, there has been a huge change in the economic system of China, and the rapid social development called for fundamental educational changes (Guo, 2013). Since then, there have been a series of educational reforms, which have exerted a significant influence on the country's basic education system. And the most unprecedented of these is the nationwide new curriculum reform which has been introduced gradually since 2000 and now covers the whole country. It dramatically changes China's traditional education in beliefs and teaching practices, especially in the teaching methods, which correlatively brings higher requirements and tremendous challenges for teachers (Brock, 2009; Guo, 2013).

2.1.1 Impact of the New Curriculum Reform

In June 2001, the Ministry of Education released *the Outline of Curriculum Reform of Basic Education (trial)* and started the New Curriculum Reform in China, which reformed curriculum standards, teaching methods and materials and evaluation systems in secondary schools. As the reform program formulated:

> *The curriculum for compulsory education must be conducive to the universalizing of nine-year compulsory education, be attainable for the overwhelming majority of the students, embody the basic requirements for citizenship, and be focused on fostering the students' motivation and ability to undertake lifelong learning. Under the prerequisite that all students should achieve the basic requirements, the curriculum for regular senior middle school has been arranged in several optional levels to give students more choices and development opportunities, and to lay a solid foundation for them to cultivate competencies in life skills, hands-on practice and creativity* (Ministry of Education, 2001).

The document specifies six aspects of changes in the curriculum (Ministry of Education, 2001). First of all, an integrated foundational education system was developed for shifting the key orientation of the curriculum to cultivate students to be lifelong learners. It also established a new structure for the curriculum to transit the traditional subject-centered structure into a more scientific and rational structure that could meet the various needs of educational institutes (Qian & Walker, 2013; Hongbiao, 2013). Additionally, some advanced theories of the curriculum were used as guidance in the reform, revising the content of the curriculum to close connect with students' lives from the difficult and complicated traditional curriculum content. Similarly, the theory of constructivist learning was significantly indicated in the reform. It emphasized using active and motivational learning methods to develop students' integrated capacities and skills rather than adopting the traditional passive and rote teaching methods (Huang, 2004). Correspondingly, appropriate evaluation and rational assessment were established to ensure the quality of classroom teaching, which required the integration of formative and summative assessment. Last but not the least, it provided democracy in the curriculum and instruction, decentralizing some free space toward the local governments and schools to administrate the curriculum (Dello-Iacovo, 2009; Qi-quan, 2006). In summary, the new curriculum reform aimed to improve the education system and fundamentally shift away from the traditional orientation. In order to make it effective, it needs teachers to participate actively (Dello-Iacovo, 2009).

2.1.2 Requirements of the Reform for Teachers

The reform has called for transformative changes in the whole Chinese education system, which put forward higher requirements to teachers, such as re-conceptualization of the value and perceptions of teaching and learning. Under such circumstances, teachers are expected to develop the relevant abilities to fully understand curriculum reform and apply them to their situations.

According to *Theory and Practice of Teacher Professionalization* (Ministry of Education, 2003), the authoritative textbook of teacher education, it put forward the requirements that teachers should have such qualities as professional knowledge, professional skills, and professional ethics. Professional knowledge, as the theoretical foundation of teacher competencies, is categorized into subjective-involved knowledge, conditional knowledge and practical knowledge. Particularly, practical knowledge is teachers' knowledge and beliefs of their individual teaching practice, and it is also the consequence of teaching experience (Van Driel, Beijaard, & Verloop, 2001). In addition, professional skills are classified into cognitive skills of teaching, operative skills of teaching and regulated skills of teaching, while professional ethics contain professional beliefs, emotions, characteristics and self-identity (Ministry of Education, 2003). All the qualities mentioned above are the professional competencies required for teachers.

2.2 Teacher Professional Development

The effectiveness of teachers is the crucial factor in the success of any education reform, which is closely connected to teacher professional development (Boyle, etc., 2004). In 2002, "*teacher professional development*" was firstly proposed by the Ministry of Education of China in the policy document *Ministry of Education's Suggestions on Reform and Development of Teacher Education During "Fifteen"* (Ministry of Education, 2002).

2.2.1 Definition of Teacher Professional Development

When it comes to teacher professional development, there is a variety of discussions of its definition among scholars, which can be categorized into two dimensions: the dynamic dimension and the static dimension. The first dimension focuses on the dynamic feature and the development process of teacher professional development. For instance, Glatthorn (1995) formulated that the professional development of teachers means the professional growth of teachers through their increasing teaching experience and the reviewing of the teaching system, while Shawer (2010) regarded teacher professional development as an ongoing improvement of professional knowledge and skills during teachers' careers. However, Hargreaves (1995) pointed out it not only refers to the development of teachers' specific aspects through teacher education or teacher training but also refers to the overall progress of teachers in the target awareness, teaching skills and the ability to work with colleagues and other aspects. Similarly, Hoyle and Megarry (2012) defined teacher professional development as the process by that teachers master necessary the knowledge and skills of professional practice in every stage of their teaching career. Therefore, although the specific definitions of the teacher professional development process among scholars are various, their key points in the perception were common, believing teacher professional development is a process of the improvement of teachers in overall aspects.

However, from the static perspective of teacher professional development, the definitions of teacher professional development are discussed in the development content. Day (2002) put forward an inclusive definition that teacher professional development includes all the natural learning experiences and the various activities by conscious organizations, which directly or indirectly benefit individuals, groups or schools, and thus improve the quality of education in the classroom. Guskey (1999) argued that teacher professional development should be the activities designed to enhance educators' professional knowledge, skills and attitudes, with the purpose of improving students' learning and study in turn. Perry (2012) formulated teacher professional development means that teachers' personal growth in professional life, including the enhancement of confidence, the improvement of skills and the constant update of knowledge of the teaching subject, as well as deepening the awareness of the reasons for teachers' behaviors in the classroom. Additionally, he pointed out that teacher professional development contains more content, which means teachers have grown into an artistic performance that is beyond the scope of skills, becoming a professional who transforms skills into authority. In conclusion, teacher professional development involves the activities and experiences that can improve teachers' qualities which lead to improvements in teaching outcomes.

Based on the functional orientation of teacher professional development, some researchers defined it from a more macroscopic perspective. For example, Hargreaves and Fullan (1992) concluded three types of teachers' development targets, regarding teachers' development as the improvement of knowledge and ability, and the development of self-understanding, as well as the revolution of ecology. These three different development orientations respectively focus on the dimensions of teachers' professional, personal and social development. The professional orientation is the most traditional, and still exerts an influence on the foundation of teacher professional development. The second type of orientation relates to the importance of personal development, which marks a significant leap in teacher development study. As for the orientation of social development, researchers (Hargreaves & Fullan, 1992) pointed out that the process and consequence of teacher development largely depend on its background and environment which may probably motivate teachers' development or inhibit it. Therefore, they suggested that with the purpose of further understanding the ecology of teacher development should be an important priority for teachers, school administrators and researchers. In addition, Evans (2002) proposed a different type of orientation in teacher development. He believed that the most significant factors for teachers' professional development are the improvement of their beliefs and attitudes, as well as their function. The development of beliefs and attitude includes intellectual development and motivation development, while the development of function focuses on the process and the outcomes of professional development.

In summary, teacher professional development can be defined as a process of continuous growth of teachers by accepting new knowledge and improving their professional ability, which includes all the activities that teachers participate in to improve their work during their careers. In this process, teachers can reach professional maturity level through continuous learning, reflection and exploration to broaden their professional content. Therefore, teachers' professional development includes not only the acquisition of knowledge and skills but also the moral and political factors in the broader context of school, society, and so on.

2.2.2 Developmental Stages of TPD

Teacher professional development contains different characteristics in different periods and stages of teachers' careers. The earliest study on the stages of teacher professional development was conducted by Fuller (1969), who believes the developmental stages of becoming a teacher are gradually progressed from concerning themselves and the teaching task to students' learning, as well as their impacts on students. He divided the stages of teachers' careers by different concerns in different periods, such as concerns about pre-teaching, concerns about early survival, concerns about teaching situations and concerns about students. However, different criteria could categorize the developmental stages of teacher professional development variously. For instance, Katz (1972) divided teacher developmental stages into survival, consolidation, renewal and maturity based on the different training needs in different periods. The survival stage is the beginning of a teaching career, mostly with a teaching experience of fewer than two years. The needs of these developmental stages may commonly be on-site support and technical assistance. The next developmental stage is the consolidation stage when teachers have taught for one to three years. At this stage, the needs of teachers' professional development would focus on on-site assistance and opportunities to access specialists, colleague advice, consultants, and advisors (Kennedy & Shiel, 2010). The third stage of professional development is the renewal stage within three or four years of teaching experience. After survival and consolidation in the career, teachers would need chances to attend conferences, professional associations, visits to demonstration projects, and teachers' centers to renew and improve themselves at this stage (Murray, 2010). Also, educational materials such as journals, magazines, and films could be the need for renewal. The last developmental stage refers to the period that teachers have taught for four to five years. At this stage, teachers tend to get maturity in a career as they need to attend educational seminars and conferences, and go to institutes to take some advanced courses or enroll in a degree program (Potthoff, Fredrickson, Batenhorst, & Tracy, 2001). Still, educational books and journals would be helpful for their professional development. Similar to this category of teacher developmental stages, Burden (1982) divided the stages of teacher career development into the period of focusing on survival, the period of focusing on adjustment and the period of maturity. He formulated there are three aspects of changes occurring in the teachers' career, including job skills, knowledge, and behaviors, attitudes outlooks, as well as job events.

However, with the developments and updates of theories and models, scholars divided the developmental stages of teacher professional development more precisely and specifically, reaching even seven or eight stages. They are more content-rich and accurate in comparison to the three or four stages in the early research. For instance, Huberman (1989) formulated seven teacher developmental stages. In the first stage, teachers focus on survival and discovery, because they are undergoing a *reality shock* and seeking methods to survive. The second stage is stabilization and the next one is experimentation, just like the consolidation and renewal stages introduced above. Teachers in these stages are more likely to get a stable situation in their careers and then have ambitions to explore new developmental opportunities. At the fourth stage which is called the *"self-doubt"* stage, teachers would experience a *"mid-career crisis"* and many of them feel monotone (Cawte, 2020; Smalley & Smith, 2017). Most of the teachers might start to get job burnout and lack of energy in professional development. The following two stages respectively are serenity and conservatism. In these stages, teachers might emerge into a worse situation of lack of energy and enthusiasm and they would more likely to reject creation and innovation (Makovec, 2018). The last stage is disengagement, which is the end of the career and teachers gradually disengage from their roles. At this stage, they mostly retired or just leave the occupation of teaching. In summary, the whole tendency of professional development is becoming more and more negative. And similar to this theory, Fessler and Christensen (1992) divided the professional development period into eight stages, including pre-service, induction, competency building, enthusiasm and growth, career frustration, career stability, career wind-down and career exit. The pre-service stage is the period when theses student teachers are still in college with some short teaching experience in their internship. The induction stage is the period when they have just entered the schools and become a new teacher (Borg, 2005). The competency-building and enthusiasm and growth stages are the periods when they get consolidation and start to seek developmental opportunities for their professional development (Callaghan, 2002). Most of the teachers have a high level of enthusiasm to improve themselves. However, after the stage of career frustration and stability, they tend to lose enthusiasm and start the wind-down stage until they finally exit the career.

Unlike these negative developmental tendencies, some researchers divided the teacher developmental stages from a more positive perspective. For example, Kugel (1993) categorized teacher professional development into five stages. In the first stage, the teacher still focuses on surviving, and in the second stage, they are more like to extend their knowledge of their teaching subject. In the third stage, they would be more advanced and start to focus on considering students' individual differences and diversity. In the next stage, teachers would focus on devising various teaching approaches, and in the last stage, they would focus on promoting independent learners. In addition, Maynard and Furlong (1995) argued that the development stages should be divided into idealism, survival, recognizing difficulties, reaching a plateau and moving on. Besides, Berliner (1994) described five stages of teacher development, respectively they are a novice, advanced beginner, competent teacher, proficient teacher, and expert teacher. Similar to this perspective, Steffy (2000) formulated six stages of teacher development, including novice teacher, apprentice teacher, professional teacher, expert teacher, distinguished teacher and emeritus teacher. These theories of developmental stages deem highly of the growth and development of teachers. In a word, no matter how the theories develop and what criteria and perspectives scholars adopt to divide the developmental stages of teacher professional development, the discernment of the early period of a teacher's career is permanent: novice teachers are on the stage of survival.

2.2.3 Characteristics of Novice Teachers' Development

As discussed above, novice teachers are at the first stage of their career, focusing on survival and basic teaching. However, as teaching is one of the most stressful jobs in service occupations (Travers & Cooper, 1996), most of the teachers, particularly novice teachers, feel stressful in teaching according to the report (Kyriacou & Kunc, 2007). All of the teachers always meet some challenges, such as lacking student engagement and behavior management, as well as lacking support for teaching (Geving, 2007; Chaplain, 2008; Davidson, 2009). As for novice teachers, they certainly meet more challenges, such as discipline and classroom management, materials assessment, instructional techniques and technology utilization, teaching pedagogy, and community involvement, as well as planning curricula and dealing with parents (Brewster & Railsback, 2001; Lundeen, 2004; Kumi-Yeboah, & James, 2012; Andrews & Quinn, 2005; Gratch, 2001; Whitaker, 2000). Among these, Fordasz and Leder (2006) argued that the top stress for novice teachers was from teaching-related activities. In Kyriacou and Kunc's (2007) report, they found that the teachers' workload was the main factor to make novice teachers feel stressed. Amador (2016) also pointed out that most of the novice teachers lacked critical noticing and thinking, just as Crutcher and Naseem (2016) formulated, many novice teachers only know '*what*' is crucial and '*how*' to do it, but they never consider beyond '*what*' and '*how*' of their teaching activities, and they don't understand '*why*' it is indispensable.

Additionally, Abbott-Chapman (2005) found that novice teachers often come across disappointment in the discrepancy between their idealized professional realization and the real situation. As Bezzina (2006) formulated, it is the transition shock caused by the novice teachers' perception of such a difference as well as lacking adequate preparation for the requirements of teaching practices. Besides, the isolated sense and the lack of support and mentoring also are the leading factors of their 'transitional shock' or 'praxis shock' in their early teaching career (Flores, 2001).

At the same time, novice teachers' development could be influenced by their individual backgrounds and contextual factors. Their working background, individual education and life experiences are significantly affecting their early teaching experiences and professional development (Flores, 2001). In the aspect of individual factors, Glatthorn and Fox (1996) stated that the factors that could influence novice teachers' professional development mostly were cognitive development factor, career development factor and motivational development factor. Hebert and Worthy (2001) also formulated that the most influential factors for novice teachers are expectations, personality, merging into the social and ability to use successful strategies in teaching. Besides, Fessler and Christensen (1992) pointed out that teachers' families, positive critical incidents, crises, individual dispositions, avocations interests and life stages are the key factors to impact novice teachers' professional development. Specifically, family as an inner supporting system for novice teachers, its members' health, welfare and financial situation may promote or block their professional development (Erdamar & Demirel, 2014; Weasmer, Woods, & Coburn, 2008). The next impact factor could be the positive critical incidents, such as sweet marriage, the birth of children, and religious beliefs. It may provide safety or a supporting foundation for a novice teacher's personal life, which can exert a positive influence on novice teachers' professional development (Weasmer et. al., 2008; Joshi, 2018). Correspondingly, a crisis, such as the sickness of a family member, the death of a friend, or loss of financial and legal dispute, could distract novice teachers' attention from teaching, and make them feel difficulty in dealing with the career pressure.

In addition to these positive and negative incidents, teachers' individual dispositions, including ambition, career goal, value, etc., could determine the decision-making skills of teachers and the developmental direction of teachers' careers (Weasmer et. al., 2008). Therefore, fully understanding the reasons for choosing to be a teacher can help novice teachers successfully overcome the obstacles in their work (Hodkinson & Hodkinson, 2004). Besides, teachers' avocations and interests could activate the intrinsic motivation for teachers to continue to develop and reflect in teaching activities, which might not only supply extra knowledge for teachers but also provide an opportunity for them to get a sense of satisfaction outside the work (Winter, 2011). What's more, what life stages the teachers were on could exert a significant influence on their individual career development. Because novice teachers are at a stage transiting into the '*adult world*' from college and beginning to take much more responsibility for individuals and society, and their personal needs and understanding of career goals are extremely different from other life stages (Poon & Lim, 2014). This is a period of exploring and experiencing, novice teachers should have enough enthusiasm and energy to adapt to the changing of their life stages (Fessler & Christensen, 1992).

In the aspect of contextual factors, Hebert and Worthy (2001) pointed out that the most influential factors for teachers' professional development could be the real situation of their working environments, as well as the evidence of impact and political culture of the schools. Moreover, Glatthorn and Fox (1996) argued that the society and community, the school system and the teaching groups or the department as well as the special activities could exert an influence on teachers' professional development. Additionally, Fessler and Christensen (1992) believed that the regulations of schools, the leadership and management style, the trust from the public, the expectations from society, and the professional organizations and unions could be the main contextual factors that influence novice teachers' development. Specifically, as teachers are restrained by the regulations of schools and communities, as well as laws of the country (Sergiovanni, 1998), these regulations and laws not only establish schools' orders and structures, but also reflect the educational goals and values of the school system and even the whole country, which would bring a sense of security to novice teachers if they could understand these regulations, and then make their professional life become more stable (Sales,

Traver, & García, 2011). Therefore, the regulations of teachers' schools could be a significant factor in deciding novice teachers' professional development (Zeichner & Tabachnick, 1985; Flores, 2004). Besides, the management style of the school leaders could exert a significant influence on teachers' individual professional careers because if a principal created an atmosphere filled with trust and support, as well as providing much more opportunities for teachers' professional development (Boylan, 2018), there would be no doubts that teachers' reflection was positive and active. On the contrary, if the leader was autocratic and dictatorial, it would definitely decrease teachers' teaching enthusiasm (Blase & Blase, 1999). Thus, the leadership and management style should be emphasized as an important factor in impacting novice teachers' professional development (Flores, 2004; Fultz & Gimbert, 2009).

Also, the public trust could deeply influence teachers' career choices and performance (Goepel, 2012). For example, if teachers were in an atmosphere filled with public trust, they would feel esteem and respect, and have adequate confidence and energies to teacher. Contrarily, if the public had been attacked and criticized for a long time, the morale of teachers would be low and even make them feel frustrated (Braxton & Berger, 1996). Hence, it is regarded as the third impact factor for teachers' professional development. Similarly, the societal expectations of schools could affect novice teachers and their development (Dinham & Scott, 2000). For instance, if society were focusing on whether schools could cultivate students to achieve high scores on tests or not, teachers would be test-oriented and pay attention to enhancing students' scores. Under such circumstances, novice teachers would focus on skills of training students to get a high score during their professional development (Wang, 2016). In addition, the other factor that influences novice teachers' professional development could be professional organizations and unions (Menekse, 2015; Hill, 2009). Because professional organizations could provide more opportunities for them to improve themselves, and the teacher unions could protect their rights and interests as well as improve teachers' working conditions. They could construct a better environment and condition for novice teachers to develop their professions (Fessler & Christensen, 1992).

In short, novice teachers always meet many challenges and dilemmas and have a desire to improve themselves. They are required to consider the needs of society, emotion, physic, learning and etc., but their own needs are often not taken into consideration (Crutcher & Naseem, 2016). Therefore, professional development programs should also consider the needs of novice teachers. Schools and the developers of teacher education programmes should lay a central concern on novice teachers' understandings and pedagogical practices (Bills, Giles, & Rogers, 2016). Gordon (2004) also stressed that professional development can help novice teachers avoid negative outcomes. However, schools should also fully consider the main factors that influenced teachers' development. Only by understanding these influential factors could schools help novice teachers to develop their profession much better.

In addition, Morris, Chrispeels, and Burke (2003) concluded the implementation of novice teachers' professional development in two ways. They are *'through external teacher networks'* and *'through internal school-reform networks'*, which contain all methods of delivery. Just as Burkman (2012) formulated, delivery is one of the most indispensable parts of teachers' professional development. Establishing external networks for teachers produce a high level of outcomes by providing a huge amount of different topics to meet *'a greater audience and a larger group of mentors or confidantes to assist in informal novice teacher induction'*, while internal networks provide efficient support and relevant training to meet the needs of novice teachers inside the school (Burkman, 2012).

2.3 Implementation of Teacher Professional Development

2.3.1 Studies on Efficient Implementations of Teacher Professional Development

There are two completely different approaches to studying the implementation of teacher professional development (Little, 2002). One of them is to research the process by that teachers master the complication of education, which is majorly focusing on the specific teaching methods or the implementations of curriculum reforms. Meanwhile, this kind of study also pays attention to exploring how teachers learn to teach and acquire knowledge and professional maturity, as well as how they maintain long-term dedication to work and so on. The other kind is focusing on the organizations or career conditions that exert an influence on teachers' motivation and learning opportunities.

In the implementation of teacher professional development, many scholars put forward some rules and principles to guarantee the efficiency of the TPD programs and strategies. For example, Gordon (2004) formulated that the efficient implementation of teacher professional development must be demonstrated by powerful leadership and evidence-based management, democracy, and cooperation among staff. He described that it should be a kind of developmental program that integrated with the existing programs and experiential learning activities embedded as a lifestyle in the schools (Gordon, 2004). In addition, Smith (2002) pointed out that the implementation should be planned well both at personal and school levels with an explicit mission and vision, and the implementation strategies should be appropriately derived from different levels of teachers with a correlative evaluation, as well as getting sustained support from different organizations including government, unions and other schools. What's more, Little (1993) pointed out that the implementation of teacher professional development should follow six crucial rules. Firstly, professional development implementation should provide ideas and materials with meaningful intellectual, social and emotional engagement both in and out of teaching. Secondly, it should clearly consider the backgrounds of teaching and teachers' experience. Thirdly, it should provide support in the informed disagreement. Fourthly, it should put classroom teaching in the larger contexts of educational careers. Fifthly, it should prepare teachers, students and parents to apply the techniques and ideas. Lastly, professional development management should guarantee bureaucratic restraint and integrate the interests of individuals and schools. Similarly, Lieberman and Miller (2001)'s argued another six principles of the implementation of teacher professional development should be that as follows. First of all, the implementation should closely center on teachers' and students' learning. Secondly, it should contain teachers' professional cooperation and corporate responsibility. Thirdly, it should establish communities for teachers to communicate, improve and be critical. Fourthly, it should encourage teachers to develop their communication skills both in oral and written. Fifthly, it should guide teachers to use structured tools and protocols to discuss. Sixthly, it should use the teaching cases from real life as the source to promote teachers' development. Moreover, Loucks-Horsley, Stiles, Mundry, Love, and Hewson (2009) stated seven principles of the implementation of teacher professional development. Firstly, it should be driven by explicit scenes of effective classroom learning and teaching. Secondly, it should provide opportunities for teachers to broaden their knowledge and improve their teaching skills, so that they can create better teaching approaches to enhance the class teaching efficiency. Thirdly, it should build a learning community for teachers to learn and share their useful experiences together. Fourthly, it should support teachers to serve in leadership roles. Fifthly, it should use model teachers to share their useful teaching strategies with other teachers. Sixthly, it should provide a connection to other parts of the educational system. Lastly, it should have continuous evaluations and assessments. Although their specific requirements are various from various, these principles of the implementation of teacher professional development all lead to the same consequence which is to ensure the improvement of teachers and the effectiveness of class teaching (Lipowski, Jorde, Prenzel, & Seidel, 2011).

2.3.2 Policy Support for the Implementation of TPD in China

Since the new curriculum reform called for higher requirements for teachers, the implementation of teacher professional development has been emphasized seriously. As the Ministry of Education (2001) pointed out, teachers should '*receive training before teaching the new curriculum*', there were some policies being issued in succession to make requirements for teacher training in response to the curriculum reform.

The Ministry of Education (2001) put forward the guidance on how to carry out the training and cultivation of teachers in *the Outline of Curriculum Reform of Basic Education (trial),* pointing out that the tertiary education institutes and other colleges and universities which undertake the training and cultivation tasks of teachers in basic education level should conduct relevant revolution in the training objectives, professional settings, curriculum structure, the utilization of teaching methods, etc., in order to adapt to the requirements of the new curriculum reform (Zhou, 2014; Zhu, 2010). A new round of basic education curriculum reform should guide the direction of continuing education for primary and secondary school teachers. The local educational administrative departments and the teacher training institutions shall formulate the specific teacher training program in which content should meet an urgent need of the new curriculum, in order to ensure the smooth implementation of the new curriculum reform (Ministry of Education, 2001). In the *2003–2007 Action Plan for Invigorating Education*, the Ministry of Education (2005) put forward that we should promote the innovation of teacher education, so as to create a new system of teacher education, especially through the implementation of '*the project of establishing high-quality teachers and management team*' to improve the primary and secondary school teachers' lifelong learning system, as well as improving the quality of teachers and management team in primary and secondary schools (Ministry of Education, 2005). In the *Suggestions of the Ministry of Education on Strengthening Teachers' Training in Primary and Middle Schools*, the Ministry of Education (2011) made the overall arrangements for a new round of primary and secondary school teachers' training work from six aspects. The first one is to attach great importance to the training of teachers in primary and secondary schools, and improve the quality of teachers. Secondly, the document focused on the central task of the development of educational reform in the new era, and carrying out integrated training for teachers in primary and secondary schools. Additionally, it emphasized the innovation of teacher training mode and the improvement of the quality of teacher training, as well as the improvement of teach training system for promoting the continuous learning and professional development of teachers. The construction of the capacity of teachers' training was supposed to be strengthened and the service system of teacher training was also suggested to be established in the document. Lastly, it pointed out that the organization and leadership of teacher professional development should be strengthened to provide a powerful guarantee for the training of teachers (Ministry of Education, 2011).

In conclusion, these documents clearly define the target and task of teacher training in the new curriculum reform (Dello-Iacovo, 2009; Zhu, 2010). It proposed new requirements in the training mode, training system, organizational guarantee and other aspects, which played an important role in promoting the development of the training for primary and secondary school teachers, as well as exerting a great influence on promoting the professional development of teachers and improving the quality of teaching and leaching.

2.3.3 Deficiencies in the Implementation under the Reform in China

However, although there were policy documents supporting teacher professional development, some reports still found that the vast majority of schools' professional development programs were not effective, and teachers did not change their views and teaching methods. Just as Dello-Iacovo (2009) formulated that many teachers were just '*simply continuing to teach as before*' in many cases. Based on a report of Shandong, Shan (2002) stated that even in the pilot project schools, although there were some student-centered activities being adopted, many teachers' teaching methods still kept as before, focusing on the textbook rather than the curriculum standards. Additionally, based on a report from Shanghai, Marton (2006) found that a huge amount of teachers were divorced from the value of new curriculum reform and persisted with the traditional teaching methods which focused on rote and memorization learning style. What's more, based on the Beijing report, Tao (2012) pointed out that many training programs departed from the actual situation and couldn't meet teachers' needs, so many of them didn't participate in the developmental program and kept teaching as before. What's more, some novice teachers even knew little about national planning documents and lacked enough understanding of them (Kravale-Pauliņa & Oļehnoviča, 2015). Therefore, in order to change a such situation, it is a priority to reform teacher education and explore efficient strategies for teacher professional development. The efficient implementation of TPD not only provides the necessary knowledge, skills, and values for teachers but also helps teachers grasp the advances in information, technology, perspectives and values in modern society (Huang, 2004). Just as Dello-Iacovo (2009) states, '*the curriculum reform should be supported by the professional development of teachers, and the teacher education reform should serve the curriculum reform'*.

2.4 Summary

In conclusion, teacher professional development, referring to the overall progress of continuous teacher training in all aspects, plays an indispensable role in educational reform. Since the new curriculum reform was introduced gradually in China, teaching teams' quality has widely aroused concern. Teachers are expected to equip with the required competencies, including professional knowledge which is consisted of subjective-involved knowledge, conditional knowledge and practical knowledge, the professional skills which contain cognitive skills of teaching, operative skills of teaching and regulated skills of teaching, and the professional ethics which involve professional beliefs, emotions, characteristics and self-identity.

As the increasing requirements bring challenges for all teachers, novice teachers who are still in the initial developmental stage of focusing on survival certainly feel much more pressure than other teachers. The main challenges they meet commonly are managing classroom discipline and routine, motivating student engagement, improving student academic achievement, dealing with student individual differences, retaining relations with parents, struggling with the heavy workload, insufficient resources and so on. Thus, the efficient implementation of teacher professional development of novice teachers is crucial.

In the implementation of teacher professional development, there are some rules and principles have been put forward. For instance, the implementation should be planned well both at personal and school levels with an explicit mission and vision, and it should also establish communities for teachers to communicate, improve and critical and it should prepare teachers, students and parents to apply the techniques and ideas and so on. These rules and suggestions provide a theoretical foundation for the actual implementation of teacher professional development. In mainland China, the ministry of education also issued some policies to introduce training models and systems for teacher professional development and made the overall arrangements for primary and secondary schools. However, there were still some reports finding that the vast majority of schools' professional development programs were not effective, and many studies on the deficiencies of the implementation have been carried out.

In a word, although the literature has provided some practical and theoretical understandings of the implementation of teacher professional development, the development of novice teachers is under-researched, especially in China. Compared with Europe and America which have already put forward some advanced concepts and development models of teacher professional development, the studies focusing on such topics in China were started much later, which led to the consequence of a much less quantity of literature, and most of the existing studies among them have been lack empirical data. Thus, this study was carried out to explore the current opportunities and needs for teacher professional development of novice teachers, with the employment of the qualitative research method.

CHAPTER THREE

Methodology

This chapter is devoted to the discussion of the methodology that this study employed. After an explanation of the reasons for employing the qualitative research approach in this study, a detailed description of the research design is put forward; this includes the design of interview questions, the procedure of the interviews, and the methods of sampling, as well as the approach of the data analysis.

3.1 The Nature of Qualitative Research Approaches

Educational research uses the scientific method to collect and analyze information systematically to promote the development of various aspects of education (Gall, Gall & Borg, 1999, p. 3). As Walliman (2010) pointed out, research methods are a range of tools that are used for different types of enquiry, just as a variety of tools are used for doing different practical jobs (p. 1). It is an indispensable and difficult responsibility for a researcher to select an appropriate and valid research method (Shulman, 1997). Generally, research methods can be categorized into two types, one is quantitative research while the other is qualitative research (Briggs, Morrison, & Coleman, 2012; Cohen, Manion, & Morrison, 2013; Denzin & Lincoln, 2000, pp. 8–10; Lodico, Spaulding, &

Voegtle, 2010; Newby, 2010; Suter, 2012; Wallen & Fraenkel, 2001; Walliman, 2010; Wiersma, & Jurs, 2009).

Quantitative research primarily relies on quantitative data collection and follows the confirmatory scientific method (Gay & Airasian, 2011; Johnson & Christensen, 2014, p. 33). It uses objective measurement and statistical analysis based on numeric data to test the hypothesis and theory (Ary et al., 2002; Gall, Gall & Borg, 2007; Johnson & Christensen, 2014). It seeks objective consequence which is more impersonal and generalizes under a specific circumstance to describe the status quo, investigate relevancy and inspect cause-effect phenomena (Gay & Airasian, 2000; Cohen, Manion, & Morrison, 2000).

In comparison, qualitative research primarily relies on qualitative data and follows the exploratory scientific method (Gay & Airasian, 2000; Johnson & Christensen, 2014, p. 33). It uses different methods like observation, interviews, and various texts to help describe points of study and comprehend people's experiences and perspectives, as well as come up with or generating new hypotheses and theories sometimes. (Denzin & Lincoln, 2008; Johnson & Christensen, 2014, p. 33). As Creswell (1994) formulated, qualitative research is "*an inquiry process of understanding a social or human problem, based on a complex, holistic picture, formed with words, reporting detailed view of the informant, and conducted in a natural setting*". It is commonly used in naturally happening situations with controlled and manipulated behaviors and settings (Wiersma & Jurs, 2009).

The qualitative research method is adopted in this research. In order to explore the opportunities and needs of novice teachers' professional development, this research needs to find out how they understand the qualities of a professional teacher and examine the challenges and difficulties they met, and probe the current strategies and programs for promoting their professional development, as well as their needs and expectations. The qualitative research method is appropriate for such kind of research which offers insights into people's thoughts, experiences and expectations and explores the "*how*" question. (Denzin & Lincoln, 2008; Gay & Airasian, 2000; Johnson & Christensen, 2014). Additionally, as listed in Chapter One, most of the research questions are essentially exploratory, such as what novice teachers require and expect in professional development, and how the schools and they themselves promote their development. Hence, the qualitative research method could help to gain insights into novice teachers' perceptions of teacher professional competence, the challenges and the development opportunities they met, as well as their current needs and expectations.

3.2 Methods of Data Collection

In educational research, the six most common methods of data collection are tests, questionnaires, interviews, focus groups, observation, and constructed and secondary or existing data (Johnson & Christensen, 2014, p. 225). Among them, as Punch and Oancea (2014) point out, *"the interview is the most prominent data collection tool in qualitative research"* (p. 144).

3.2.1 Interviews

An interview is an effective approach to "accessing people's perceptions, meanings, definitions of situations and constructions of reality" (Punch & Oancea, 2014, p. 144). It is a process occurring under a face-to-face circumstances to get the needed information or data verbally through communication or interaction (Koul, 1997). According to the degree of control, there are three kinds of interviews: structured, semi-structured, and unstructured interview (Holstein & Gubrium, 1995; Koul, 1997). The structured interview has little room for the varied responses as the pre-established questions and pre-set response categories are used. On the contrary, the unstructured interview is a "non-standardized, open-ended, in-depth interview, sometimes called ethnographic interview." (Punch & Oancea, 2014, p. 147). Between these two types, the semi-structured interview is guided by interview questions structuration but follows all the principles of an unstructured interview. In case of going too far beyond the scope of the topic, it asks structured questions with an interview guide and then explores more deeply to get valuable information by asking open-form questions (Gall, Borg, & Gall, 1996, p. 310).

For the purpose of answering the research questions, the needed data is in terms of the following aspects: the novice teachers' perceptions of professional competence and the difficulties they met, the implementation of programs and strategies for promoting novice teachers' professional development, the novice teachers' needs and expectations for teacher professional development, and so on. In order to collect these data, this research adopted the in-depth interview method, which was recognized to collect in-depth information about an interviewee's subjective feelings, knowledge, opinions, reasoning, beliefs, and motivations (Johnson & Christensen, 2014, p. 233). Besides, the interviews adopted a semi-structured type to dig out more useful information under the range of the topic by using the interview protocol.

3.2.2 Interview Questions

For the semi-structured interview, the researcher designed a series of interview questions to facilitate the answering of the four main research questions:

> Q1: What are the novice teachers' perceptions of teacher professional competence?
> Q2: What challenges and difficulties have the novice teachers met? And how do these difficulties influence them?
> Q3: What programs and strategies are adopted to promote novice teachers' professional development?
> Q4: What are the needs and expectations of novice teachers for continuous teacher professional development?

As mentioned in Chapter One, Q1 intended to probe whether novice teachers have a will to improve themselves, and what professional competencies of teachers pursue to develop. Therefore, the first two questions listed below were used to know about interviewees' opinions of occupation and their career motivation:

> Q1.1: How do you think about the teachers' occupation?
> Q1.2: Why did you choose to work as a teacher?

After these warm-up questions, the researcher continued to dig out the interviewees' perceptions of professional competencies and what qualities they want to develop:

> Q1.3: What qualities do you think an excellent teacher should have?
> Q1.4: What aspects do you need to improve?

In the above Chapter One, Q2 wanted to know about what challenges and difficulties novice teachers have met and whether these difficulties exerted a negative influence on them. Hence, the corresponding interview questions were designed as followings:

> Q2.1: What are the biggest challenges and difficulties you met before? And how did you overcome it?
> Q2.2: What are your greatest confusions and needs at present? Have you ever had job burnout?

As Q3 was set to examine the current strategies and programs for promoting novice teachers' professional development in school and how the teachers promoted themselves, the interview questions were set like that:

- Q3.1: As a novice teacher, how do you adapt to classroom teaching and enhance your teaching quality?
- Q3.2: Have you subscribed to any educational reading materials? What are they?

These two questions mentioned above were used to find out how novice teachers developed themselves and whether they had the initiative in professional development. And the next two questions were set to examine how schools promoted novice teachers' development and whether they were effective.

- Q3.3: Please introduce your school's promoting strategies and programs.
- Q3.4: What do you think of the effectiveness of these strategies?

The rest of this part was asked to dig out whether there was a motivated relevance between schools' reward system and teachers' initiative in professional development.

- Q3.5: Do you participate in any self-paying training program? What are they?
- Q3.6: Have you carried out any research projects since you took the post? Can you provide any examples?
- Q3.7: Is there any reward system for teachers' professional development in your school? Any examples?

The next three questions were used to examine the efficiency of the promoting strategies and programs from schools and individuals.

- Q3.8: What are the main sources of help that promote your professional development as we talked about above?
- Q3.9: What are your major gains from these development opportunities?

After gaining factual information, Q4 was to get insight into novice teachers' needs and expectations for professional development.

- Q4.1: Are you satisfied with the current situation?
- Q4.2: What is your expectation in teacher professional development?

The last two questions were asked to know about novice teachers' needs and expectations in their professional development, which will help to conclude the efficient strategies for promoting teacher professional development.

Although all the interview questions mentioned above were set by different categories according to the research questions, the actual interviews did not need to strictly follow this sequence, as there were some same categories of information could be revealed among different categories of interview questions. For instance, interview question Q1.4 indicates the same category of information as the research question Q4. As these interviewees are Chinese, all the interview questions were asked in Chinese.

3.2.3 Interview Procedure

All the interviews were carried out one on one and recorded by audio devices for subsequent transcriptions. The researcher followed the advice of Grosvenor and Rose (2001) to guarantee a good quality audio recording, such as choosing a well-furnished room to absorb echoes, turning off the mobile phone to avoid unwanted noised, checking the devices with enough power and memory space before the interview (p. 113).

During the process of interviews, the researcher kept a good manner to build up a friendly atmosphere and using eye contact in the response. Just as Ma and MacMillan (1999) formulated, the interviewers should establish a positive rapport with participants to make them feel comfortable enough to openly and completely answer the interview questions. In order to make the interviews easier, the researcher used Chinese to communicate with the interviewee although this article is written in English. Before the interview, the interviewee received a list of the research questions in advance which was also typed in Chinese to know about the procedure of the interview and the main content of the research.

3.3 Sampling

A sample is a set of elements selected from the population based on the specific rules to which the researchers try to generalize the consequence. (Johnson & Christensen, 2014; Wiersma & Jurs, 2009). In the process of sampling, researchers need not only to decide which people to interview but also to consider settings and processes (Punch & Oancea, 2014, p. 162). They should select samples on purpose from which they can get a full comprehension of the phenomena under the qualitative study (Ritchie, Lewis, Nicholls, & Ormston, 2013, pp. 77–80). As for the types of sampling, Wiersma and Jurs (2009) concluded that there are four kinds: stratified random sampling, cluster sampling, systematic sampling, random sampling, and purposeful sampling. Johnson and Christensen (2014) classified there are eight types of sampling: simple random sampling, systematic sampling, stratified random sampling, cluster random sampling, convenience sampling, quota sampling, purposive sampling, and snowball sampling. This study adopted purposeful sampling or called purposive sampling, which is defined as choosing the individuals who have the features that the researcher specifies from a population of interest (Johnson & Christensen, 2014).

As the research topic focused on novice primary school teachers' professional development, this research selected 12 novice primary school teachers from 6 different provinces in China. The six provinces were Guangdong, Zhejiang, Anhui, Jiangxi, Yunnan, and Gansu. These provinces have implemented the new curriculum reform in all primary and secondary schools since the autumn of 2005 (Ministry of Education, n.d.).

All the interviewees graduated from the same faculty of a normal university. They have gained about one year of teaching experience since graduation, so they have a similar pre-service academic background and are equipped with relatively the same level of theoretical foundation in education. The major difference between them is their working backgrounds. The specific information of the interviewees is shown in Table 3.1.:

Table 3.1 Information of the interviewees

NO.	Interviewees	Gender	Province	Area
T1	Miss. Li	Female	Anhui	urban
T2	Miss. Huang	Female	Jiangxi	rural
T3	Miss. Xu	Female	Jiangxi	urban
T4	Miss. Bai	Female	Gansu	Urban
T5	Miss. Li	Female	Guangdong	Urban
T6	Miss. Yang	Female	Zhejiang	Urban
T7	Mr. Cheng	Male	Zhejiang	Rural
T8	Miss. Zhang	Female	Jiangxi	Rural
T9	Mr. Lai	Male	Yunnan	Rural
T10	Miss. Shen	Female	Guangdong	Urban
T11	Miss. Li	Female	Guangdong	Urban
T12	Miss. Li	Female	Yunnan	Urban

As the description in the above table, some of them teach in urban areas while others do in rural areas. These different factors of their work backgrounds might lead to different professional development results among teachers.

3.4 Data Analysis

Methods of data analysis should be systematic, controlled, transparent, and described (Punch & Oancea, 2014, p. 173). As Wiersma and Jurs (2009) formulated, *"Analysis in qualitative research is a process of successive approximations toward an accurate description and interpretation of the phenomenon"* (p. 237). There are several approaches to analysis, such as grounded theory analysis, narrative analysis, ethnomethodology analysis, conversation analysis, discourse analysis, semiotics, documentary analysis, and phenomenological analysis (Punch & Oancea, 2014). In order to extract and analyze the needed information from the conversation of the interview recordings, the researcher needed to transform the audio materials into transcripts with codes. Just as Punch and Oancea (2014) pointed out, *"Coding is the starting activity in qualitative analysis, and the foundation for what comes later"*, and they believe coding is the core to directly analyzing and discovering the regularities of the collected data. In the aspect of coding methods, Saldaña (2015) divided its sections into First Cycle and Second Cycle coding approaches:

> *The portion of data to be coded during First Cycle coding processes can range in magnitude from a single to a full paragraph to an entire page of text to a stream of moving images. In Second Cycle coding processes, the portions coded can be the exact same units, longer passages of text, analytic memos about the data, and even a reconfiguration of the codes themselves developed thus far.* （p.3）

In this study, the researcher firstly identified the codes from the data and then combined similar codes. For instance, the data under the codes of "working stability", "high social status", "working environment" were grouped as theme "career motivation"; "subject knowledge", "teaching skills", "professional ethics" were integrated as "professional abilities"; "training courses", "lesson with heterogeneous", "experience-sharing meeting", "teaching research workshop", "rewarding system" were labeled as "promotion strategies in school level"; "seeking help from experienced teachers", "self-paying training program participation", "educational reading materials subscription", "doing research project" "reflection" were sorted as "self-improvement strategies"; "improvement in classroom management", "improvement in students outcomes", "useless" were classified as "effectiveness of promoting strategies"; "active emotional feedback from students ", "self-denying",

METHODOLODY | 31

"heavy working burden", "job burnout", "confusing about future" were marked by "feelings"; "needs of mentoring", "will of teaching skills improvement", "higher salary", "improvement of school facilities", "chances of trying various teaching methods" and "needs of more training programs" were tabbed as "expectation". The process of coding is shown in the following intercepted fragment of a specific example (Figure 3.1):

Figure 3.1 Intercepted fragment of coding 1&2

After two cycles of coding, the interview data were categorized into the following four dimensions:

(a) Novice teachers' perception of TPD;
(b) Challenges for novice teachers;
(c) TPD opportunities for novice teachers
(d) Current needs and expectations for TPD.

Through categorizing data in these dimensions as emerging themes, analyses were further elaborated on the multilevel connections of these themes before addressing the research questions in light of these themes and arriving at the conclusions.

3.5 Limitations of the Study

This research employed the qualitative research method, interviewing 12 novice teachers as the study samples, and brought useful findings and implications about teacher professional noticing for novice teachers. However, the study still has some limitations.

Due to the nature of qualitative research approaches, this research is not objective as it gains insights into people's thoughts, experiences, and expectations (Denzin & Lincoln, 2008; Gay & Airasian, 2000; Johnson & Christensen, 2014). The data were collected and analyzed without objective measurement and statistical analysis. Therefore, subjectivity can't be eliminated as one of the inherent characteristics of qualitative research.

Additionally, the sample size of this study is very small, and the adopted sampling method is purposeful sampling rather than random sampling. The findings are based on the 12 teachers selected from the 6 provinces, which may not be the generalization of the overall situation in mainland China. As Boyce and Neale (2006) formulated, the results of the in-depth interviews are not generalizable because small samples are selected and random sampling is not employed.

Despite the inherent lack of subjectivity and the generalizability of this study, the researcher expects the findings can resonate with readers, especially for those who are under similar circumstances and face the alike situation. In this way, it could provide a reference for them to acquire a deeper understanding of novice teachers' professional development.

CHAPTER FOUR

Findings and Analysis

This chapter sets out the findings and analysis in terms of novice teachers' perception of the qualities of a professional teacher, the challenges they have met in teaching, as well as the opportunities offered by multi-level providers that can promote their development. Ending with the needs and expectations of notice teachers for their teacher professional development, this chapter analyzes the findings in light of the literature based on the collected interview data. As mentioned in Chapter Three, the study involved 12 interviewees from different provinces.

4.1 Background of the Interviewees

This research adopted a qualitative research methodology, using in-depth semi-structured interviews to dig out the needed information to answer the research questions. Using purposeful sampling, 12 novice primary school teachers from 6 provinces of China with about 1 year of teaching experience were selected as interviewees. The six provinces were Guangdong, Zhejiang, Anhui, Jiangxi, Yunnan, and Gansu. As the table of the interviewees' information showed in the last chapter, the researcher chose three interviewees from Guangdong and Jiangxi respectively as well as two from Zhejiang and Yunnan respectively, and the last two novice teachers were chosen from Anhui and Gansu. What's more, four of the interviewees are working in rural areas while the rest eight teachers work in urban areas. In summary, one-quarter of the participants are working in Guangdong while the other quarter is from Jiangxi. The same proportion of participants is indicated between Yunnan and Zhejiang, as well as between Anhui and Gansu, occupying 17% and 8% respectively. In addition, most of the participants are working in the urban cities, occupying 67%, while the rest 33% of them are working in the rural areas.

As all the interviewees graduated with a bachelor's degree in education from the same department of a normal university at the same time, they had similar teacher education backgrounds and received similar theoretical knowledge in education through core courses. The obvious differences among them were their working environment revealed in the above pie charts, which exert an influence on the situation of interviewees' professional development. Besides this external background, their professional value also affects their working attitude and development spirit. Thus, the beginning question of the interviews was set to explore novice teachers' career motivation.

Career motivation, influenced by the situation, and manifested in career decisions and behaviors, is regarded as a multidimensional construct that is internal to the individual (Noe, Noe, & Bachhuber, 1990). The effect factors of career motivations can be divided into internal factors and external factors. External factors are from the objective world such as the characteristics or features of the occupation, while the internal one is from the subjective world of the interviewees like individual personality or interest.

In the aspect of external motivation, based on the interview data, three dominative factors drove interviewees to choose to work as a teacher, including stable employment, high social status, and professional training.

The employment status of teachers is very stable in mainland China, especially in public schools. Because of the Chinese teachers' policy system, the teaching staff establishment policy of primary and secondary school directly ensure the status and rights of teachers (Hang, Peng, & Xie, 2010). It is rare for teachers to worry about unemployment or take a large pay cut because of unfavorable market conditions. Thus, many interviewees deemed it as a crucial factor attracting them to be a teacher, especially female teachers.

> *… I chose to be a teacher because … There are several factors. The first one is the work is stable.*
> *(T1 Miss. Li, Anhui)*

> *I think this occupation, cultivates people, huh. In fact, I do not want to do this work, just thinking the work is relatively stable …*
> *(T2 Miss. Huang, Jiangxi)*

> ... *As a girl, we all feel that this job is very stable, and there are two good holidays.*
> *(T5 Miss. Li, Guangdong)*

Additionally, teachers have a high social status. Because in Chinese culture, one of the traditional virtues is to respect teachers. Just as Fwu and Wang (2002) formulate, the Chinese cultural tradition has exerted an influence on forming the relatively high social status of teachers. Therefore, it has become another factor to attract interviewees.

> ... *The social status is pretty good, the most important thing is that I think the environment is relatively simple and pure. Ah, I quite like it.*
> *(T1 Miss. Li, Anhui)*

> ... *I think this occupation in China is a traditionally high social status, and sometimes, when you teach some kids, they will have some heartfelt love, gratitude, and so on towards you ...*
> *(T5 Miss. Li, Guangdong)*

> *This occupation is respected. Its social status is very good. For example, when I took the driver's license course, the coach knew that I am a teacher and then he took more care of me.*
> *(T6 Miss Yang, Zhejiang)*

Moreover, as all the interviewees majored in education in the same normal university, working as a teacher is consistent with their undergraduate major. According to a survey report on the employment situations of 1100 normal university graduates from 5 higher education institutions in China, most of the normal graduates plan to devote themselves to their educational career, occupying 73.8% of all responders (Tu & LI, 2005). Therefore, some of the interviewees chose to teach because they received professional training in this job. Just as some of them described:

> ... *and the other reason is, I did not find the other work. Because my major is education, I can only choose this way.*
> *(T2 Miss. Huang, Jiangxi)*

> *The reason why I want to be a teacher, first of all, is that this job is consistent with my major.*
> *(T7 Mr. Cheng, Zhejiang)*

> *Being a teacher is because I majored in this profession.*
> *(T12 Miss. Li, Yunnan)*

Besides these three common factors, there are still some other reasons to be a teacher. For instance, some interviewees believe the working environment of educators is very pure in comparison with businessmen or politicians. Some interviewees think it is very attractive that teachers have a long summer holiday and winter holiday, and the other interviewee chose to be a teacher because of their family support.

In the aspect of internal motivation, most of the interviewees consider choosing to be a teacher because they love children and enjoy teaching them.

> *This work brings me feelings of freshness. Staying with children and teaching them, is a very happy thing for me.*
>
> *(T3 Miss. Xu, Jiangxi)*

> *Well, I think the most important thing for me is the students! Because I prefer to deal with children, I think the children in school are very cute. … although they sometimes make me angry. But most of the time they are pretty good. They're really cute.*
>
> *(T6 Miss. Yang, Zhejiang)*

Similar to this reason, some interviewees consider that it can increase their sense of achievement after teaching the children.

> *… And sometimes, when you teach some kids, they will have some heartfelt love, gratitude, and so on towards you, which will really increase a person's sense of accomplishment …*
>
> *(T5 Miss. Li, Guangdong)*

> *The first reason is that I will have a sense of accomplishment seeing them progress …*
>
> *(T10 Miss. Shen, Guangdong)*

Besides, there are still some effect factors of internal motivation, such as believing the job is suitable for their personal character, regarding teaching as a challenging job, or thinking it can make her rich in soul.

4.2 Perception of Qualities of Professional Teacher

As all the interviewees are normal graduates, they have learned the basic educational knowledge in the same university, and have already formed the educational theoretical framework. Although their different experiences shaped their perception framework individually, most of their answers are still similar in understanding the content of teachers' professional competencies. In their opinion, professional knowledge, professional skill, and professional ethics are the three crucial professionalism of a good teacher. According to *Theory and Practice of Teacher Professionalization* (Ministry of Education, 2003), the general textbook of teacher education, professional competence also be classified into these three dimensions; they are professional knowledge, professional skills, and professional ethics.

Professional knowledge, as a set of practice-oriented and complex understandings, plays an important role in shaping and directing teachers' work (Elbaz, 1983). All the interviewees believe that professional knowledge is an indispensable component of the professionalism of an excellent teacher. Just as one of them pointed out:

> ... Professional quality, I think it can be divided into two parts. The first part is your own professional knowledge. ... if a child asks you a question but you do not know how to answer, they will have a sense of distrust of the teacher. Certainly, the efficiency of class teaching will be reduced a lot, which can have a great impact on the teaching effect.
> (T5 Miss. Li, Guangdong)

Others also hold the same attitude toward professional knowledge. Take some descriptions for instance:

> The most important thing about being a teacher is that his professional knowledge must be solid. You should have something in your brain before you hand it over to the students.
> (T6 Miss Yang, Zhejiang)

> A good teacher must have the personal professional knowledge, right? Then classroom management is also very important ...
> (T7 Mr. Cheng, Zhejiang)

In addition, most of the interviewees argue that professional skills are another key component of the professionalism of an excellent teacher. As Kyriacou (2007) formulates, the essence of being an effective teacher depends on the teaching skills which are defined as the discrete and coherent activities that teachers use to foster student learning, including planning and preparation, lesson presentation, lesson management, classroom climate, discipline, assessing pupils' progress and reflection and evaluation.

> To be a good teacher, the most critical competence is professional ability; the second one is the ability of teaching and learning ...
> (T1 Miss. Li, Anhui)

> I thought the main competencies are knowledge and ability, which is very simple to comprehend and do not need to explain.
> (T4 Miss. Bai, Gansu)

> ... Another part is teaching skills, which is also important ...
> (T5 Miss. Li, Guangdong)

> ... The second point is the teaching skills because if you don't know how to teach, it will be useless ...
>
> (T6 Miss Yang, Zhejiang)

Professional ethics, as Koocher and Campbell (2016) point out, it is the foundation of any profession because it is important for those who serve the public to assume responsibility. From the point of the interviewees' views, professional ethics is also regarded as a necessary component of professionalism that is the top priority in a teacher's professional competence. They described it as "love", "patience", "responsibility", "conscience" and "morality". The following are some interviewees' descriptions.

> ... the last essential one is about love and patience ...
>
> (T1 Miss. Li, Anhui)

> ... However, after being a teacher, what I felt more important than these is a moral quality.
>
> (T4 Miss. Bai, Gansu)

> I think there are a lot of excellent teachers' characteristics. First of all, I think it must be better to be patient ... Secondly, I think it really needs to have a sense of responsibility ... Additionally, it also needs to be conscience ...
>
> (T5 Miss. Li, Guangdong)

> ... In addition, your character should be good because there are so many people in the world! Children are looking at what you say and what you do. If you don't do it as a norm, you cannot talk about teaching.
>
> (T6 Miss Yang, Zhejiang)

In conclusion, although the career motivation varied across the interviewees, their career decisions were dependent on four factors: stability of the career, high social status of the job, major of education, and the love of children. In comparison, their views on the professional competencies of an excellent teacher are more similar, including professional knowledge, professional skills, and professional ethic.

Figure 4.1 Professional competencies of teachers

4.3 Challenges for Novice Teachers

As novice teachers, they certainly meet some challenges and sometimes feel frustrated (Fantilli & McDougall, 2009). Based on the model mentioned above, challenges for the interviewees can be categorized into these three dimensions: professional knowledge, professional skills, and professional ethics.

4.3.1 Challenges in Professional Ethics

Ethical issues always appear in situations where judgments are made difficult by conflicting demands (Koocher & Campbell, 2016). It is difficult for teachers to discern the ethical factors involved in teaching due to the various goals and tasks (Colnerud, 1997). From the collected data, interviewees sometimes encounter two dilemmas about whether they should resist private supplement tutoring and take kickbacks.

In both the public school system and private school system, there is a widespread global phenomenon called private supplementary tuition in that teachers to provide paid educational tuition services to school children beyond normal school hours, which is on a significant increasing trend (Kwok, 2010; Chui, 2016). In mainland China, daytime teachers are officially prohibited from providing private supplementary tuition to their daytime students, but based on the data of the Social Survey Institute of China, there are still more than 60% of public school teachers in major cities conducting private supplementary tutoring with their daytime students during summer or winter vacations (Kwok, 2010). Inevitably, novice teachers are also involved in this "*Shadow education system*".

> … *The second point is that our teachers' incomes are considerable. That is because we can tutor students, and although it gets out of line, we still can do that. Ha-ha, I just now tutored students. Normally in primary school, it is to spend one more hour to stay with students. This kind of income is much higher than our wages.*
>
> *(T7 Mr. Cheng, Zhejiang)*

This interviewee accepts the matter without hesitation, while the others are not so sincerely to accept such private supplementary tuition.

> *I have received some requests from parents asking me to tutor their children privately. But as a new teacher struggling for survival, I don't have the extra vigor to do this. I know the payment will be remarkable, but that is breaking the rule of our education bureau. I know teachers in my office are doing such things, but I don't know whether I can keep rejecting them in the coming years.*
>
> *(T10 Miss. Shen, Guangdong)*

I am tutoring some students after class in my home, that is not illegal and every teacher does so. But if you provide tutoring in school, it will be dangerous because you cannot make sure whether there is nobody reporting you. Anyway, I going to tell you the dilemma is that some parents of those students I am tutoring want me to treat their children better than other students, but I don't like to do that ...

(T11 Miss. Li, Guangdong)

Taking kickbacks means when schools or grade groups need to purchase learning materials for students, teachers will get kickbacks from the dealers, which is also illegal. In comparison to private supplementary tuition, taking kickbacks is much more hidden as an unspoken rule. As an interviewee exposed:

You know any career will have a problem with taking kickbacks once it involves purchases. At first, I didn't know why I get an extra bonus from the grade group without reasons, then I found every teacher in this grade also get the bonus, so I asked and they told me that was kickbacks of exercise books. I felt angry but I didn't know what to do. Can I report that? They are my dear fellows. Can I reject the bonus? They will suspect I am going to report them.

(T8 Miss. Zhang Jiangxi)

4.3.2 Challenges in Professional Skills

The dominant part of novice teachers' challenges emerges in the dimension of professional skills. Fantilli and McDougall pointed out that (2009) the main challenges of novice teachers are managing the behavior and diverse needs of students, time constraints, and workload, as well as conflict with parents and other adults. Similarly, the interviewees complain that they are suffering from analogical difficulties, including managing classroom discipline and routine, motivating student engagement, improving student academic achievement, dealing with student individual differences, retaining relations with parents, as well as struggling with a heavy workload and insufficient resources and support.

Classroom management is a high-priority concern for novice teachers (Wubbels, 2011). It is also a crucial factor in deciding whether a teacher could build a positive learning environment (Hue & Li, 2008). As poor classroom management exerts a negative influence on teaching and learning activities, it has become the main cause of teacher stress (Friedman, 2006). Just as some interviewees complained:

In my teaching, the biggest challenge and difficulties are class discipline and class performance. When I first came to this class, the discipline is not good. I shouted hoarsely, but the children do not listen to me and conducted a variety of slapstick.

(T1 Miss Li, Anhui)

> *The biggest challenge is classroom management. As I am a kind girl, my students are not afraid of me. Last week, the headmaster came to obverse my class and then he said my classroom is too noisy and told me to improve discipline.*
>
> *(T3 Miss Xu, Jiangxi)*

> *For example, I am not familiar with classroom management. That is, management of student discipline …*
>
> *(T12 Miss Li, Yunnan)*

In addition, poor student engagement is another problem for novice teachers. Engagement is composed of students' synchronous concentration and cognitive immersion and their interest and enjoyment in a teaching and learning practice (Strati, Schmidt, & Maier, 2017), which is regarded as an indispensable role that playing in students' personal development and academic success (Hawkins, 2015). As novice teachers, interviewees find it really hard to stimulate student engagement.

> *The biggest difficulty and challenge is that I cannot activate the atmosphere of the classroom. It is a kind of lifeless, as the students did not enter the classroom.*
>
> *Well, I have asked others (senior teachers) for help, but there is still no good method to resolve it. The atmosphere is so difficult to activate because the math lesson is very boring and it doesn't have so many activities …*
>
> *(T2 Miss Huang, Jiangxi)*

> *Another challenge is that sometimes students in my classroom don't engage in my teaching.*
>
> *(T5 Miss. Li, Guangdong)*

Besides student engagement, student achievement is also widely viewed as a critical challenge for teachers (Strati, Schmidt, & Maier, 2017). Under the test-oriented circumstance, student academic achievement has been regarded as a crucial evaluation standard for teachers. As facing the poor classroom management and student engagement, novice teachers inevitably have problems in improving student academics achievement.

> *… The class I am teaching do not perform well in academic achievement. According to a number of tests, I think its academic results should be in the countdown of the whole grade. Because the discipline of my class is not good, they do not listen to my teaching, so the academic results are certainly poor and it is hard to be raised.*
>
> T1 Miss Li, Anhui

> *In fact, I am so worried about the academic results of our class can't be improved. We are almost ranked in the countdown of the grade group in each test.*

> *These children do not listen carefully in my class, and every time the rank of the academic score comes out, I feel very embarrassed.*
>
> T10, Miss Shen, Guangdong

There is no doubt that poor classroom management and student engagement will lead to unsatisfactory student academic achievement. However, sometimes a teacher who can maintain a good learning atmosphere is still facing such challenges. Just as one of the interviewees complain,

> *The knowledge I had taught several times in the classroom, was understood by the children at that time, and they also solved the exercise by themselves. But strangely, after two days, they couldn't solve the same exercise.*
>
> T9, Mr. Lai, Yunnan

As students have their individual learning style which is different from each other (Germain & Scandura, 2005), how recognizing students' individual differences and then conducting specific education, has become a challenge for novice teachers.

> *At present, the greatest challenge I encountered is when I face so many students, it comes up with problems about how to know about their individual difference, how to discover their strengths, and how to develop their personalitieas, as well as cultivate their moral characters.*
>
> T4 Miss. Bai Gansu

What's more, many interviewees complain that they lack enough resources or support in teaching, which is regarded as a challenge for them, especially in the rural area.

> *I seldom seek help from these experienced teachers, because they are not willing to help us, and some of them are even not willing to let us visit their classes.*
>
> (T2, Miss Huang, Jiangxi)

> *My school is really lacking such a chance that you can freely conduct the teaching activities which you have learned.*
>
> (T5 Miss. Li, Guangdong)

> *I'm doing a research topic about the integration of math and science classes in elementary school because my school gave me this task. However, I cannot find any information or literature on this topic, I surfed the Internet but still found nothing, even in the CNKI.*
>
> (T7, Mr. Cheng, Zhejiang)

Additionally, many novice teachers complained their workload is excessive, which should be highly emphasized because the problems of excessive workload problems force many novice teachers to leave the profession in their first years of teaching

(Butt & Lance, 2005). According to the interviewees, most of them are suffering from an excessive workload.

> … I am very busy. I have a lot of things to do. Sometimes I need to teach physical education lessons and moral lessons. Sometimes I also need to help other teachers to substitute them for teaching lessons. I have so many miscellaneous things to do …
>
> (T3, Miss Xu, Jiangxi)

> Firstly, our teaching task is really excessive. As if almost all teachers are busy in teaching every day in each semester. We don't have extra time, to carry out a full activity.
>
> (T5 Miss. Li, Guangdong)

> Teachers' working time is longer than other units. Civil servants go to work at half past eight, but our primary school students start class at eight o'clock, which means we have to reach school before half past seven o'clock, so we have an hour earlier every day than others.

> … We novice teachers are assigned much more tasks to do than these senior teachers. Such activities like teaching symposiums, all are assigned to us new teachers. Normally all the activities in our school are done by us, new teachers. We have a lot of things to do every day. We are so busy that we have to work overtime usually.
>
> (T7, Mr. Cheng, Zhejiang)

> I have so much work to do at school. I feel dizzy when I am off duty every day. As you see, I am still working overtime now.
>
> (T12, Miss Li, Yunnan)

Moreover, some of the novice teachers found it difficult to keep good relations with parents. As home-school cooperation has become a heat issue of education, keeping good relations and communication with parents is important for teachers. However, some interviewees meet the challenge on this issue.

> I need to improve the skill of communication with parents. As parents have a deeper and richer social experience than me, I should put myself in the teacher's angle and height, so as to give parents more professional advice.
>
> (T5 Miss. Li, Guangdong)

> So, I think it is difficult to deal with the parents. Sometimes some parents talk with me on the phone for about half a day, saying their children's situation at home, sometimes I am really very busy and I don't want to continue the conversation. But I feel embarrassed to interrupt their speech, which is really bothering me a lot.
>
> (T11 Miss Li, Guangdong)

However, as some of the interviewees assume the duty of a class teacher who should be in charge of various class routines, they find it difficult to manage routine.

> ... Another challenge is that I don't know how to train students' routines, such as their writing habits, speaking methods in the class and so on.
>
> *(T3, Miss Xu, Jiangxi)*

> When I suddenly took over the class as a class teacher, I felt a bit mentally disturbed, especially when I can't arrange the routines well. I really do not know what to do and when to do it. The routines include homework, home visits, class meetings, attendance records, various programs, helping students who have learning difficulties, and so on.
>
> *(T8, Miss Zhang, Jiangxi)*

Besides these eight mainstream challenges mentioned above, there are also some minority difficulties in the professional skills of novice teachers being reflected in their needs and expectations, which are revealed in Section 4.5.

4.3.3 Challenges in Professional Knowledge

Professional knowledge is categorized into subject-related knowledge, practical knowledge, and conditional knowledge (MoE, 2003). As these interviewees have been professionally trained in their undergraduate university, they don't have many problems with subject-related knowledge. But in the aspect of practical knowledge and conditional knowledge, they meet challenges.

Practical knowledge is teachers' knowledge and beliefs of their individual teaching practice, and it is also the consequence of teaching experience (Van Driel, Beijaard, & Verloop, 2001). As those novice teachers lack enough teaching experience, some of them are certainly worried about this.

> ... I am lacking this kind of knowledge, such as how to manage the classroom, and how to use the teachers' language to express somethings. Our university hasn't taught this practical knowledge.
>
> *(T12 Miss. LI, Yunnan)*

Conditional knowledge is classified as a kind of knowledge in long-term memory that knowing when to use declarative and procedural knowledge correctly under a specific condition (Bruning, Schraw, Norby, & Ronning, 2004). However, as novice teachers do not teach long enough, they lack such kind of knowledge in the long-term memory of teaching.

> ... I need to develop a method of speaking, because I always don't know whether I should talk in a specific situation. I feel in this aspect I may not be as normal as another person. And I also need to strengthen my specialties ...
>
> *(T2 Miss. Huang, Jiangxi)*

FINDINGS AND ANALYSIS | 45

I feel frightened if there is an incident occurring because I don't know how to deal with it. As dealing with the problems like students' fighting in class is easy, but if a student suddenly dizzies during an activity, it will make me so worried. Last time the loss of my student really scares me, I search for him street by street with his mother ...

(T10 Miss. Sheng, Guangdong)

As these challenges are categorized into three dimensions which aim at the three different levels of professional competence, based on the Figure 4.1 of professional competencies of teachers, it can be summarized in a figure of challenges for novice teachers as shown in the following Figure 4.2:

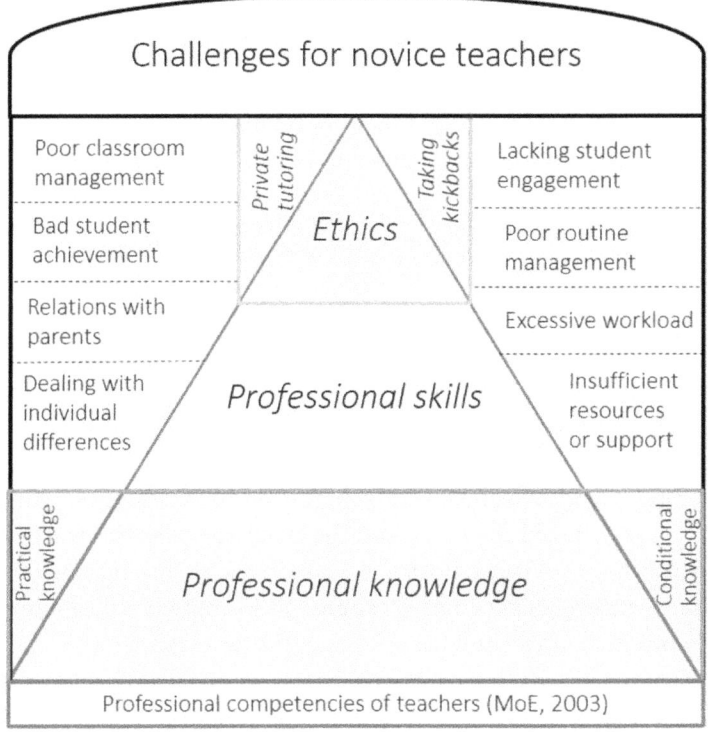

Figure 4.2 Challenges for novice teachers

4.3.4 Negative Outcomes of the Challenges

As Fantilli and McDougall (2009) pointed out, challenges and difficulties make novice teachers feel like failures, these interviewees also produce some negative emotions, such as self-denial, fatigue and job burnout. These negative emotions are mainly caused by poor classroom management and excessive workload.

Classroom management, as the dominant challenge for most of the novice teachers, it also attributed the most to their negative outcomes.

> *I have job burnout, which is a feeling that I don't want to teach lessons and a strong feeling of tiredness. That is because those students don't fear new teachers and sometimes I can't hold the discipline …*
>
> *(T2, Miss Huang, Jiangxi)*

> *Job burnout makes me feel like there is not much room for improvement. And in aspects of classroom management, I feel it have no good method to resolve it …*
>
> *(T4 Miss. Bai Gansu)*

> *… In order to attract the attention of students, the methods I adapt are not just using activities, sometimes I still have to shout, which makes me feel that I am really failed.*
>
> *(T5 Miss. Li, Guangdong)*

Excessive workload is the other nightmare for novice teachers, especially in urban areas. They complain there is always so much work being assigned to them.

> *… I have 14 classes a week, quite a lot. There are three to four classes a day on average, which makes me feel really tired. Additionally, our wages are relatively low, so I have burnout.*
>
> *(T1 Miss Li, Anhui)*

> *I have job burnout and I think the pressure is really excessive. I did not know teachers have so much pressure before …*
>
> *(T3, Miss Xu, Jiangxi)*

These negative emotions depress teachers a lot, and sometimes it will exert an influence on teaching quality, which should be highly emphasized. As a matter of fact, all the problems mentioned above, are also the heat issue of novice teachers around the world, which have aroused scholars' and educators' attention for years. In order to improve novice teachers' situation, there are some programs and strategies being carried on to promote novice teachers' professional development.

4.4 Current Opportunities for TPD of Novice Teachers

These programs and strategies used to promote the teacher professional development of novice teachers can be categorized into three different levels, including state level, school level, and individual level. Among them, schools play the most indispensable role in offering opportunities for novice teachers to develop.

4.4.1 School Programs of Promoting TPD for Novice Teachers

According to the interviewees, although there are various promoting programs and activities conducted by the school, they can still be concluded into four main methods: lesson observation and evaluation, teaching symposium, training programs, as well as the mentoring system.

Lesson observation and evaluation is the most common method that the school adopts. It is always implemented in the two following forms: class observation and heterogeneous of the same lesson. Class observation is in the most widespread use in schools, consisting of two different directions. The first direction means that novice teachers go to visit the class of a senior teacher, learning how to teach effectively from the observation. Oppositely, the second direction is for the senior teachers to come to observe the class of a novice teacher, and then make some comments and suggestions on the teaching.

> *We have lesson evaluations, but not usually, approximately once per month. Lesson evaluation is an "open course", which means that a teacher teaches a lesson and then other teachers evaluate it after visiting the class.*
>
> *(T1 Miss Li, Anhui)*

> *Another method is to let the other teachers observe my class, pointing out the advantages and disadvantages, just like the matter that the principal visited my class as I mentioned.*
>
> *(T3, Miss Xu, Jiangxi)*

The other form is heterogeneous of the same lesson, called "*Tong Ke Yi Gou*" in Chinese. It is an activity in that all teachers in the same grade group teach the same lesson in their own methods, and then they can learn from each other through lesson observation. Just as one of the interviewees described:

> *Every week we will have an activity called the heterogeneous form of the same lesson, which is to organize teachers from the same grade and the same subject group to teach the same lesson. I feel its effectiveness is much better because it is aimed at teaching skills.*
>
> *(T4 Miss. Bai, Gansu)*

Besides lesson observation and evaluation, a teaching symposium called "*Jiao Yan*" in Chinese is also adopted generally. There are always some groups in schools taking charge of the teaching symposium, organizing some activities to help novice teachers promote their teacher professional development by cooperative learning, such as collective lesson preparation, group discussion on teaching, and teaching seminars. Discussion on teaching is a usual method used to communicate with the opinions of the reflection on a lesson among teachers.

> ... We have a teaching symposium activity ... For example, if this semester is the North district of our town takes charge in the teaching symposium, all the English teachers of our district will go to a specific school. After that, the teachers from the North district will have several lessons and then we will discuss these lessons ...
>
> (T6 Miss Yang, Zhejiang)

> ... Teaching symposium, in our math group, is where one teacher teaches a lesson and other teachers in the math group all come to observe this class and then discuss on it ...
>
> (T7, Mr. Cheng, Zhejiang)

Sometimes schools also invite some famous educationalists, experienced teachers or the representative teachers to deliver lectures for novice teachers.

> ... Such as our school, if we have six English teachers, it only sends a representative of each subject to go out to learn, and then they convey their experiments to us after coming back. But most of the time, we don't get much from this activity.
>
> (T4 Miss. Bai, Gansu)

> Additionally, some teachers will deliver lectures to share their teaching experiences in the seminars.
>
> (T5 Miss Li, Guangdong)

In addition to lesson observation and evaluation, and teaching symposium, offering some training programs for novice teachers is regarded as another crucial method to promote teacher professional development, which can be classified as offline training and online training. The content of training offline could be various from various. Besides aiming at enhancing novice teachers' teaching qualities, some training programs are even set to improve their physical and mental situation, such as the Tai Chi training course, and moral values training program which are pointed out as follows.

> As for extracurricular training, I have participated once computer training which was arranged by our school. And it also offered us a Tai Chi training course.
>
> (T1 Miss Li, Anhui)

> At the beginning and the end of each term, our school has a big training program in terms of moral values for all the teachers and students.
>
> (T5 Miss Li, Guangdong)

Based on the collected data from the interviews, online training programs are only offered in urban areas, some of the schools even deem it as a compulsory task for novice teachers.

> ... We have a regulation that teachers must have specific learning hours online. We can choose the interesting online courses offered by the teaching symposium center ...
>
> (T5 Miss. Li, Guangdong)

Meanwhile, mentoring is also widely adopted in schools as an effective way in promoting novice teacher professional development (Salleh & Tan, 2013). Some interviewees' schools have systematic mentoring, while some only simply assign a senior teacher for the novice as a mentor.

> ... My headmaster assigned a mentor for me. I observed a lesson of her, and then imitated her to teach the same lesson in my class. So I always taught one lesson later than her. I was taught hand by hand, but she only taught me in the first month ...
>
> (T3, Miss. Xu, Jiangxi)

> We have a mentoring called "Shi-Tu in Pairs" which is to assign a senior teacher to mentor new teachers ...
>
> (T12, Miss. Li, Yunnan)

Compared with this kind of mentoring that just simply assigned a senior teacher for novice teachers, the following schools provide a more systematic mentoring that the mentoring time lasts much longer and a specific bonus also be given to the mentors as motivation.

> We have the mentoring system which is a senior teacher mentor new teachers. We call it "Qinglan" project.
>
> (T6, Miss. Yang, Zhejiang)

> ... Our school assigns a mentor for us who is a teacher within three years. For instance, if you are a math teacher and then the school will assign a senior teacher to mentor you in how to teach math, and you can learn from him for any teaching skills. We call it "Qinglan" project and the mentor will get the specific bonus ...
>
> (T7, Mr. Cheng, Zhejiang)

4.4.2 Individual Strategies for Promoting TPD

Although schools have made a significant contribution to teacher professional development of novice teachers, there are still some aspects that schools can't refer to, such as novice teachers' individual differences, which can only be supplied by themselves.

Based on the collected data, as most of the interviewees have a strong wish to improve themselves, they have explored some individual strategies for promoting their own professional development, which can mainly be concluded as four different approaches, including seeking help from senior teachers, getting resources from the internet, taking online courses, and self-reflection.

For some of the novice teachers, seeking help from senior teachers is the straightest and the most convincing method to get the answers to the problems.

> *... We have three classes in a grade, the other two teachers are quite experienced in teaching. Although they are not my mentors, I always consult them if I meet something I don't understand, such as how to teach a tiny exercise ...*
>
> (T1 Miss Li, Anhui)

> *... I usually communicate with the experienced teachers, and sometimes I also discuss some issues with my peers, which can let me get a lot of inspiration ...*
>
> (T4 Miss. Bai, Gansu)

> *... I consult experienced teachers for lesson plans and visit their classes ...*
>
> (T9 Mr. Lai, Yunnan)

From the points of the above interviewees, they can learn experience from senior teachers and then improve themselves.

However, although seeking help from senior teachers is the most convincing method, there is no doubt that the senior teachers are not omnipotent, so this approach still has some limitations. As a new generation in this information era, those novice teachers have their own advantage in information retrieval. They can get the resources they want from the internet, even in the rural areas.

> *Improving teaching competence mainly depends on myself, such as watching online videos.*
>
> (T2, Miss Huang, Jiangxi)

> *I also surf the internet, such as collecting some useful methods and experience of classroom management.*
>
> (T4 Miss. Bai, Gansu)

> *I search on the internet for some teaching cases which are the real teaching practices. And then I will reflect on the methods to improve myself after comparing the differences between my teaching and others.*
>
> (T5 Miss Li, Guangdong)

Similar to the approach mentioned above, some interviewees also pursue their professional development through the internet. However, the biggest difference between taking the online course and getting resources from the internet is that they get a systematic training rather than scattered information. For example, some interviewees take open online courses.

> ... I also search for some open online videos of courses that I am interested ...
>
> *(T9 Mr. Lai, Yunnan)*

Besides taking such free courses, some interviewees also register for self-paid online courses to improve themselves.

> ... I have registered for a self-paid online course for a certification exam. It contains totally 48 hours of training courses and I have to finish it in my spare time every weekend ...
>
> *(T11 Miss. Li, Guangdong)*

In addition, self-reflection is regarded as the most important strategy in individual development by the interviewees. Some of them even believe it contributes the most to their teacher professional development, just as the following transcribes reveal.

> *The improvement of teachers' competence, is mainly attributed by self-reflection of my class teaching.*
>
> *(T1 Miss Li, Anhui)*

> *It mainly relies on my self-reflection. There is no other way because no one is willing to teach me how to do it, I have to grope slowly by myself.*
>
> *(T2, Miss Huang, Jiangxi)*

> *Most of the time, I reflect on myself, combining it with my own learning experience, to improve gradually.*
>
> *(T4 Miss. Bai, Gansu)*

> *The most important method is self-reflection. After teaching a class, I summarize and reflect on myself in time, and then I can improve my teaching in the next class, which makes me improve continuously.*
>
> *(T6, Miss. Yang, Zhejiang)*

4.4.3 State Programs of Promoting TPD for Novice Teachers

As the influence of novice teacher professional development exerted by the state is imperceptible, in comparison to the school programs and the individual strategies, the state seems to play a less critical role in TPD of novice teachers. Only several interviewees can straightly point out the program implemented by the state or education bureaus. The key methods that the state adopted to promote teacher professional development are through the reward system and training programs.

According to the interviewee, the reward system is mainly consisted of professional title evaluation and paid training. Teacher professional title evaluation is very important for teachers, and the state uses it to motivate teachers to improve themselves. For instance, some education bureaus formulate that the research publications of novice teachers can add the score to their professional title evaluation.

> ... If you have some research publication, you will have priority in the promotion of evaluation of professional titles ...
>
> (T2 Miss. Huang, Jiangxi)

Paid training is used to motivate and improve teachers. For example, if novice teachers' working year reaches a specific number, they can apply for a paid training.

> ... The reward is also issued by the Education Bureau. The content of the reward is that if you have already worked for a specific number of years, you will be eligible to apply for paid training which means that your tuition will be paid by the Education Bureau and you can still get half of the salary ...
>
> (T5 Miss Li, Guangdong)

State also some provide some training programs for teachers, and most of them are large-scale in comparison to school training programs.

> ... Our school seldom organizes training for us teachers. Mostly we can go for a training is because of the requirements of superiors such as the Bureau of Education, or the national training program ... Sometimes, for example, if we have to go out to participate in a short-term training, which costs generally about a day, or a half-day, normally we should adjust the lessons in advance and arrange the students well before going out ...
>
> (T4 Miss. Bai, Gansu)

> Our teaching symposium group of the education bureau will also organize some teachers' training. For example, last year I participated in a 90-hour training. Now there is a credit system for teachers in our province, which is regulated that only the teachers who receive specific credit points within three years can be considered qualified ...
>
> (T6, Miss. Yang, Zhejiang)

In short, all these opportunities offered by the state, schools, and individuals are set to help novice teachers to overcome their difficulties and challenges. Combining with the Figure 4.2 of challenges for novice teachers, it can be extended as the following figure (Figure 4.3):

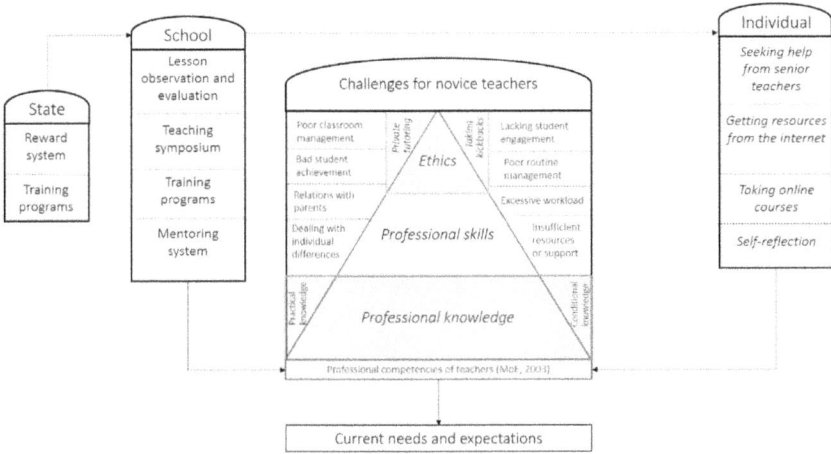

Figure 4.3 Current opportunities in teacher professional development

4.5 Current Needs and Expectations

Although there are many various programs and strategies offered for novice teachers to develop their profession, they still have some needs and expectations. Continually based on the three levels mentioned above, novice teachers' needs and expectations can also be categorized into these three dimensions, including expected support from the state and school, as well as expected improvement in personnel.

4.5.1 Expected Support from the State

In the expected support from the state, interviewees are straightforward, hoping the education bureau to raise teachers' salaries and issue some policies to improve their welfare situations.

> … I think our wages should be raised. We are really hard-working but only get so little wages every month …
>
> (T3, Miss. Xu, Jiangxi)

> … I just hope the welfare offered by the education bureau can be better and better.
>
> (T6, Miss. Yang, Zhejiang)

4.5.2 Expected Support from the School

As for schools, interviewees have more specific needs, such as hoping the school to assign them a mentor, provide more professional development opportunities, equip them with necessary teaching facilities, and provide the independent option.

Most of the interviewees whose schools have no mentoring system wish their school can assign a mentor for them, such as one of them describes:

> … it would be much better if there is a mentor to me and who can often guide me.
> (T1 Miss Li, Anhui)

Besides, many of them are not satisfied with their current situation and are eager to have more opportunities to improve their professional development. They need more chances to learn and grow up.

> *Additionally, the opportunities for teacher training and communication are not enough, that is the expectation for the school.*
> (T1 Miss Li, Anhui)

> *… because our school is in the countryside, the opportunity for learning is very little, basically, there is no any chance …*
> (T2 Miss Huang, Jiangxi)

> *… I hope our school can provide us with more professional development opportunities, the more practical, the better.*
> (T4 Miss. Bai, Gansu)

In rural areas, some interviewees complain that the facilities situations in their schools are not complete to guarantee their teaching qualities.

> *My school is a good school with hundreds of history, but the teaching facilities are not satisfying compared with the primary school I stayed in before. For example, although our school has an electronic board, but its function is not complete …*
> (T1 Miss Li, Anhui)

The worst situation is that the school even lacks the basic facilities, which inevitably decreases the teaching quality.

> *The facilities in our school are really old and out of date. As we are in the countryside, the condition is very awful. Many tubes and fans in the classroom are broken, and there is only one computer in a grade. I hope my school can improve these necessary facilities.*
> (T8 Miss. Zhang, Jiangxi)

Moreover, as newcomers to an organization often burden with more odd jobs and run errands, novice teachers may suffer this in schools. For example, one of the interviewees complains his school always assigns jobs to him straightly without any discussion. He hopes to have the right to choose what to do and not to do.

> ... Our school's leadership style is different. If there is an activity need to be arranged, the school leaders will straightly order a teacher to take charge of it, without any discussion. So, I hope we can have right to choose something, instead of directly assigning a task to us.
> (T7, Mr. Cheng, Zhejiang)

4.5.3 Personal Goals for Future Development

When it comes to the expectation in the personal level, the eventual goal of novice teachers is to be successful. Most of the interviewees wish they improve their individual professional competence, such as learning more professional knowledge, improving teaching skills, and being respected and loved by students. As lifelong learning is becoming a more and more heated issue, many novice teachers wish to learn more professional knowledge.

> *I hope to improve my professional knowledge ... As there is a gap between my major and the teaching subject, I have to spend more time on grasping the teaching content ...*
> (T5 Miss. Li, Guangdong)

> *... Professional knowledge. For example, as teaching in an elementary school and their knowledge is very simple, you will slowly ease up on yourself, you will forget a lot of knowledge, such as some English words. So I think, teachers should keep learning so that they can keep up with the pace of time and continually deliver new knowledge to students.*
> (T6, Miss. Yang, Zhejiang)

In addition, teaching skills as the part where novice teachers meet the most challenges, they certainly have a strong wish to improve it.

> *I think there are no any special requirements, mainly in terms of work. I hope my teaching ability can have a significant improvement ...*
> (T1 Miss Li, Anhui)

> *In the aspect of classroom management ... I hope I can control the discipline by using eyes, without talking about anything.*
> (T7, Mr. Cheng, Zhejiang)

Meanwhile, in many interviewees' perceptions, being loved and respected by their students is regarded as one of the necessary symbols of a successful teacher.

I expect to be a teacher that students love, not just having a fun with them or the laughing kind. That is a kind of relative respect …

(T2 Miss Huang, Jiangxi)

I hope that my students will not hate the subject because of me. It will be the beat If they can enjoy this subject because of me. I hope they can learn in happiness and interest, that is my biggest wish.

(T11 Miss Li, Guangdong)

In short, in the expectation of the support of the state, the interviewees hope to raise their salaries and provide them better welfare; in the expectation of the support of the school, they wish decision-makers can establish a mentoring system for novice teachers and provide more professional development opportunities for them to learn. Additionally, they suggest schools should be equipped with necessary teaching facilities to ensure the teaching quality, and the leaders had better provide the independent option for teachers. From the aspect of the individual, it still bases on the professional competence of teachers. They hope they can improve their professional knowledge and teaching skills, as well as be an admirable teacher respected and loved by students.

CHAPTER FIVE

Discussions and Conclusions

In this chapter, the findings are discussed deeply in light of the literature in Chapter Two, and the ideas revealed from these findings are also developed and theorized. Four parts of the findings responding to the four research questions about teacher professional competence, novice teachers' challenges, teacher professional development opportunities and novice teachers' expectations are explored, and the differences between rural and urban areas are also discussed. Additionally, this chapter put forward the implications and ends with the conclusion of the significant issue of this research.

5.1 Summary of Findings

Novice teachers seemed to hold a strong value towards teacher identity, exerting a positive influence on their professional development and their belief in professional knowledge, professional skills and professional ethics as the core aspects of teacher professional competence. Challenges to novice teachers' individual teacher professional competence are accordingly analyzed and categorized in these three aspects, while the strategies they found and the changes they expected at the individual, school and state levels are tabulated and depicted in Table 5.1.

Table 5.1 A synthesis of multi-level analysis of findings

Level	Professional Ethics		Professional Skills		Professional Knowledge	
Individual	Challenges		Challenges		Challenges	
	Private supplementary tutoring; Taking kickbacks		Classroom management; Student engagement; Student academic achievement; Dealing with individual differences; Insufficient resources and support; Excessive workload; Relations with parents; Routine arrangement		Practical knowledge; Conditional knowledge	
	Strategies adopted	Changes expected	Strategies adopted	Changes expected	Strategies adopted	Changes expected
	Self-reflection	Be respected and loved by students	Seeking help from senior teachers; Getting resources from the internet; Self-reflection	Improve teaching skills	Taking online courses; Self-reflection	Learn more professional knowledge
School	Professional Ethics		Professional Skills		Professional Knowledge	
	Measures offered	Expected support	Measures offered	Expected support	Measures offered	Expected support
	Training programs; Mentoring system	Independent option	Lesson observation and evaluation; Teaching symposium; Mentoring system	More professional development opportunities; Teaching facilities	Training programs; Mentoring system	Mentoring
State	Reward system	Higher salary and better welfare	Training programs	More professional development opportunities	Training programs	Mentoring system

Negative emotions such as self-denial, fatigue and job burnout developed when novice teachers faced difficulties and challenges including classroom management, excessive workload, student engagement, student academic achievement, dealing with individual differences, insufficient resources or support, relations with parents and routine arrangement, among which the first two were most common.

In order to overcome these difficulties, teachers adopted strategies to improve themselves, such as seeking help from senior teachers, getting resources from the internet, taking online courses, and self-reflecting. Schools also promoted opportunities for teacher professional development, such as programs on lesson observation and evaluation, teaching symposiums, training programs, and mentoring systems. At the state level, there is a national training plan and reward system in professional title evaluation and paid training programs. Comparing the impacts at various levels on teacher professional development, mentoring in schools was regarded most effective program, while self-reflection as the most effective individual strategy.

However, these programs and strategies did not always satisfy the needs of novice teachers. While all anticipated more development opportunities to improve their professional competence, some hoped the school could provide more independent options for teacher professional development and improvements in teaching facilities to ensure teaching quality. A higher salary and better welfare offered by the education bureaus were found crucial to raise the morale and status of teachers.

5.1.1 Teacher Professional Competence

The novice teachers in this study were found to hold similar perceptions of teacher professional competence because they had similar teacher education backgrounds as well as a similar theoretical foundation in education through core courses. They generally believed that teacher professional competence comprises of knowledge, skills and ethics, as this is stated in *Theory and Practice of Teacher Professionalization* (Ministry of Education, 2003), the authoritative textbook of teacher education. According to the normative framework in this text by the Ministry of Education, teacher professional competence covers professional knowledge, professional skills and professional ethics (Ministry of Education, 2003). Specifically, professional knowledge includes personal knowledge, conditional knowledge and practical knowledge, while professional skills of teachers comprising of cognitive skills, operative skills and regulated skills of teaching. Professional ethics broadly embrace professional beliefs, emotions, characteristics and self-identity.

Novice teachers' perceptions of professional competence may determine the direction of their professional development. Enhancing the professional competence of teachers may lead to the higher congruence between teachers' perceptions of their professional competence and their perceptions of professional satisfaction (Friedman & Faber, 1992). Case studies on Hong Kong teachers by Tang and Choi (2004) showed that an international field experience in a teacher education programme with the language and cultural immersion would enhance preservice student teacher's professional competence through situated professional learning experiences. This implies that teachers not only can learn the theoretical knowledge about teacher professional competence through textbooks, but also can develop their professional competence in teacher education programmes.

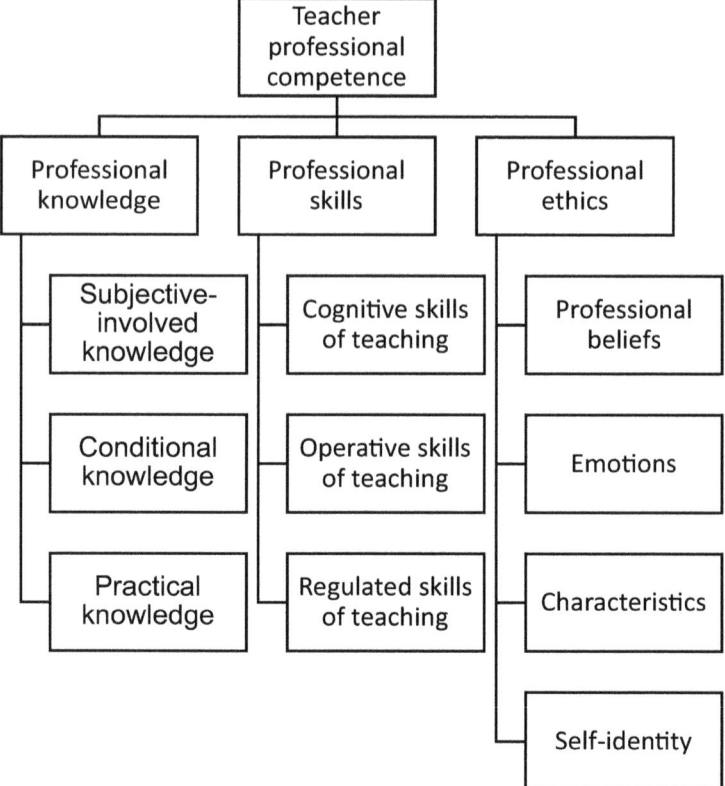

Figure 5.1 Framework of teacher professional competence

5.1.2 Challenges and Negative Outcomes

Novice teachers meet many difficulties during the early years of their teaching career (Onafowora, 2005). Even if they have developed their professional competence to some extent in teacher education programmes, they inevitably have to face challenges in many aspects, such as discipline and classroom management, materials assessment, instructional techniques and technology utilization, teaching pedagogy, and community involvement, as well as planning curricular and dealing with parents (Brewster & Railsback, 2001; Lundeen, 2004; Kumi-Yeboah, & James, 2012; Andrews & Quinn, 2005; Gratch, 2000; Whitaker, 2000). Among these, teaching-related activities and the workload are often regarded as the main challenges that make novice teachers feel stressful (Forgasz & Leder, 2006; Kyriacou & Kuncs, 2007).

Contrary to the general belief that Chinese teachers do not have classroom management as their western counterparts, novice teachers in this study had difficulties in classroom management and student engagement. In addition, they had to boost student academic achievement, deal with individual differences, and insufficient resources and support, and cope with excessive workload in increasing demands from parents and administrative routines. These difficulties lead to negative outcomes such as self-denial, fatigue and job burnout for teachers, and among which poor classroom management and the excessive workload were almost unbearable.

Novice teachers are at a stage transiting from school to '*adult world*' where they have to shoulder much more responsibilities as well as individual needs that require a firm understanding of career and life goals (Fessler & Christensen, 1992). Disappointments arise when the discrepancy between their idealized professional realization and the real situation is unresolved (Abbott-Chapman, 2005). This transition shock occurred when novice teachers could not reconcile the differences between ideals and reality and lacked adequate preparations for the demands of teaching practices (Bezzina, 2006). They are expected to have sufficient enthusiasm and energy to withstand the changes in their new life stages (Fessler & Christensen, 1992). If they cannot overcome the negative impact exerted by the 'transitional shock', they may be disillusioned or depressed, compromising their teaching accomplishments (Fantilli & McDougall, 2009). Many teachers left the profession for various reasons in the first three years after graduation from teacher education programmes (Fantilli & McDougall, 2009). Therefore, supporting novice teachers to face difficulties and dilemmas should be priorities in the teacher professional development agendas of schools and the state, and methods of helping them face the challenges should be put forward.

5.1.3 Development Opportunities

Successful professional development opportunities for novice teachers can help them avoid the negative outcomes (Gordan, 2004). It cannot only strengthen the knowledge, skills and dispositions of individual teachers as well as the overall teaching quality of the school, but also exert a significant positive effect on students' performance and learning (Villegas-Reimers, 2003).

Professional development opportunities for novice teachers were found multilevel, including at the state level, the school level, and the individual level. At the Individual level, novice teachers adopted strategies to improve themselves individually, such as seeking help from senior teachers, getting resources from the internet, taking online courses, and self-reflecting. At the school level, mass programs were set by individual schools to promote teacher professional development of novice teachers. Common topics of these school programs include lesson observation and evaluation, teaching symposiums, training programs, and mentoring systems. At the state level, a national training plan with paid training programs and a formal reward system with professional title evaluation were regarded as popular measures to support teacher professional development. These programs and strategies aiming at the improvement of teacher professional competence are concluded as follows:

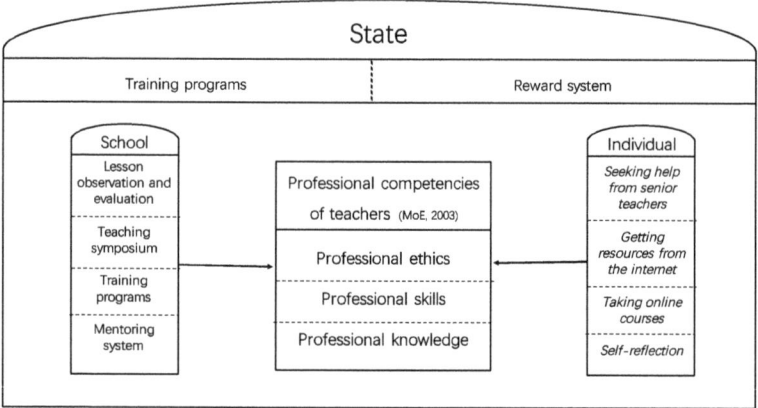

Figure 5.2 Teacher professional development programs and strategies

In the current findings, although the state seemed to play a less critical role in promoting teacher professional development of novice teachers, its invisible influences on schools and teachers were overarching and fundamental. Compared to the state and individual level impacts, schools often contributed stronger and more durable impacts on teacher professional development. Among the four programs offered by schools, the most significant one was mentoring, because experienced teachers can help novices succeed at the early teaching stage (Feiman-Nemser, 2001). Mentoring program is regarded as a vehicle to support and retain novice teachers (Huling & Resta, 2001). It plays a crucial role in increasing the retention of novice teachers in the teaching profession (Kajs, 2002). It can also benefit mentor teachers substantially in their professional competency, reflective practice, renewal, psychological benefits, collaboration, teacher leadership and so on (Feiman-Nemser, 2001).

Compared with school programs, novice teachers' individual strategies were more flexible in catering to individual needs with varied effectiveness. Among the four common strategies novice teachers adopted, self-reflection was the most significant. A critically reflective stance toward teaching can help teachers overcome demoralization and self-laceration (Brookfield, 1995). It is proposed more and more as a crucial characteristic, sometimes even a defining quality of excellent teaching (Elbaz, 1988). It has been regarded as an ongoing process and a routine part of teaching (Richards & Lockhart, 1994). As Donnelly and Fitzmaurice (2011) point out, self-reflection is one of the most contributory factors in teacher developmental activities. Thus, there would be no doubt that teachers' reflection was positive and active.

5.1.4 Needs and Expectation

Teachers are required to consider the physical, emotional, social and learning needs of students, but their own needs are often not taken into consideration (Crutcher & Naseem, 2016). However, teachers' personal needs should be emphasized because their professional growth is closely dependent on whether their individual needs are addressed in professional development programs they took (Lee, 2005).

Like the strategies adopted and changes expected, needs of novice teachers' needs were categorized at three levels. At the individual level, novice teachers are expected to learn more professional knowledge, improve their teaching skills, and earn respect and love from students, implying a strong desire for quality professional development. At the state level, teachers expected not only a higher salary and better welfare, but also measures to narrow the gaps between the education provisions in urban and rural areas. At the school level, many teachers expected needs and support from senior colleagues, suggesting strong demand for professional mentor schemes. The classroom facilities in some schools also needed upgrades to support teaching and options for professional development needed to be broadened to cater to individual needs. The management style of the school leaders is also considered to exert a significant influence on individual teachers' career development (Fessler & Christensen, 1992). A principal who can create a school climate full of trust and support is more likely to provide more opportunities for teachers' professional development. On the other hand, if the principal was dominating and authoritarian, the enthusiasms of teachers might be lowered. While teachers' working background can significantly affect their early teaching experiences and professional development (Flores, 2001), school leaders should consider creating a better working environment for teachers.

5.1.5 Differences between Rural and Urban Areas

With the gap in economic development between the urban and rural areas widened, the differences in education provisions have emerged prominently. This regional inequality in the provision of public education has made teachers face a lack of access to transportation, cultural resources, or educational facilities (Zhang & Kanbur, 2005; Sargent & Hannum, 2005).

According to the current findings, the challenges and needs of novice teachers reflect the rural and urban differences in three aspects. Firstly, the rural teachers lacked sufficient resources and support and they were eager for professional development opportunities more than the urban teachers. That is because the city-oriented policies have imposed an unfair allocation of public education resources favoring the cities (Chuanyou, 2006).

In addition, there is a significant difference in occupational opportunity and wages difference between rural migrants and urban residents (Meng & Zhang, 2001), and many teachers in rural areas expect a higher salary and better welfare. Moreover, school conditions for rural residents were much worse than their urban counterparts (Zhang & Kanbur, 2005). Some novice teachers in rural areas complained that their schools lack basic teaching facilities to guarantee the classroom teaching.

In short, teachers serving in rural areas face more difficulties in professional development, and a better understanding of the ways to support rural teachers can help promote access to quality education for children there (Sargent & Hannum, 2005). Policymakers should consider distributing public educational resources fairly and strategically to narrow the gap in compulsory education between urban and rural areas (Chuanyou, 2006).

5.2 Implications

The findings of this research suggest three directions for the development of future teacher professional development. First, more training on classroom management and time management is indispensable as poor classroom management and excessive workloads were the main causes of novice teachers' burnout. Teacher educators and school leaders are suggested to offer more practical training for novice teachers to grasp essential classroom management skills and to assign reasonable workloads to avoid burnout.

Second, school leaders and policymakers should set up a mentoring program in schools to support novice teachers. As the mentoring programs can substantially benefit both novice teachers and their mentors (Huling & Resta, 2001), they may be more effective than many other teacher professional development opportunities. Third, more development opportunities for teachers in rural areas are required to improve their professional competence. A fair and rational distribution of public educational resources may narrow the rural and urban gaps.

5.3 Conclusion

In mainland China, higher professional requirements have been imposed on teachers since the launch of the new curriculum reform in 2001. As a result, novice teachers face a set of challenges given that they are at the stage of struggling for survival with limited experience and achievement. Under the teacher professional development policies introduced by the Ministry of Education, education bureaus and schools have paid more attention to developing effective development programs for novice teachers.

This study explored novice teachers' perceptions of teacher professional competence as well as the challenges and development opportunities operated at multi-level. Their current needs and expectations were also explored. This research adopted qualitative research methodology using interviews of 12 selected novice primary school teachers from 6 provinces at different implementation stages of the new curriculum reform. The findings showed that there was no significant difference among provinces in teacher professional development, but the development opportunities in rural areas were much more limited than those in urban. Compared to state and individual-level professional development opportunities, mentorship in schools contributed the most to teacher professional development. The study also indicates self-reflection of novice teachers was prominent in individual differences in teacher professional development strategies. Poor classroom management and excessive workload were the main causes of novice teachers' burnout, but more development opportunities are expected to improve their professional competence. Higher salaries and better welfare are crucial for maintaining a stable supply of quality teachers.

For teacher educators and school leaders to make the decision, the current findings provide empirical evidence on the relative impact of different professional development measures as well as implications on best practices to support novice teachers to further their own professional development and enhance their teaching quality. The evidence is expected to enrich the theories of teacher professional development.

References

Abbott-Chapman, J. A. (2005). Let's keep our beginning teachers. *Principal Matters: The official journal of the Secondary Principals' Associations of Australia*, Summer 2005, 2–4.

Amador, J. (2016). Professional noticing practices of novice mathematics teacher educators. *International Journal of Science and Mathematics Education*, 14(1), 217–241.

Andrews, B. D. A., & Quinn, R. J. (2005). The effects of mentoring on first-year teachers' perceptions of support received. *The Clearing House: A Journal of Educational Strategies, Issues and Ideas*, 78(3), 110–117.

Ary, D., Jacobs, L. C., & Razavieh, A. (2002). *Introduction to Research in Education*. Wadsworth Group: CA.

Avalos, B. (2011). Teacher professional development in teaching and teacher education over ten years. *Teaching and Teacher Education*, 27(1), 10–20.

Berliner, D. C. (1994). Expertise: The wonder of exemplary performances. In John N. Mangieri and Cathy Collins Block (Eds.), *Creating powerful thinking in teachers and students* (pp. 141-186). Ft. Worth, TX: Holt, Rinehart and Winston.

Bezzina, C. (2006). Views from the trenches: Beginning teachers' perceptions about their professional development. *Journal of In-Service Education*, 32(4), 411–430.

Bills, A. M., Giles, D., & Rogers, B. (2016). " Being In" and "Feeling Seen" in professional development as new teachers: The ontological layer (ing) of professional development practice. *Australian Journal of Teacher Education*, 41(2), 106–121.

Blair, D. V. (2008). Mentoring novice teachers: Developing a community of practice. *Research Studies in Music Education*, 30(2), 99–117.

Blase, J., & Blase, J. (1999). Principals' instructional leadership and teacher development: Teachers' perspectives. *Educational Administration Quarterly*, 35(3), 349–378.

Borg, M. (2005). A case study of the development in pedagogic thinking of a pre-service teacher. *Tesl-Ej*, 9(2), n2.

Boyce, C., & Neale, P. (2006). *Conducting In-Depth Interviews: A Guide for Designing and Conducting In-Depth Interviews for Evaluation Input*. Pathfinder International. Monitoring and Evaluation, 2, 1-12.

Boylan, M. (2018). Enabling adaptive system leadership: Teachers leading professional development. *Educational Management Administration & Leadership*, 46(1), 86–106.

Braxton, J. M., & Berger, J. B. (1996). Public trust, research activity, and the ideal of service to students as clients of teaching. *New Directions for Institutional Research*, 1996(90), 79–91.

Brewster, C., & Railsback, J. (2001). *Supporting Beginning Teachers: How Administrators, Teachers and Policymakers Can Help New Teachers Succeed*. Northwest Regional Educational Laboratory's Information Services.

Briggs, A. R., Morrison, M., & Coleman, M. (2012). *Research Methods in Educational Leadership and Management*. (3rd ed. / edited by Ann R.J. Briggs, Marianne Coleman & Marlene Morrison.). London: Sage Publications.

Brock, A. (2009). Moving mountains stone by stone: Reforming rural education in China. *International Journal of Educational Development*, 29(5), 454–462.

Brookfield, S. (1995). *Becoming a Critically Reflective Teacher*. San Francisco: Jossey-Bass.

Bruning, R. H., Schraw, G. J., Norby, M. M., & Ronning, R. R. (2004). *Cognitive Psychology and Instruction* (M. Harlan & A. Crisp, Eds., 4th ed.). Upper Saddle River, NJ: Pearson Education.

Burden, P. R. (1982). *Developmental Supervision: Reducing Teacher Stress at Different Career Stages*. Paper presented at the Annual Meeting of the Association of Teacher Educators (Phoenix, AZ, February 15, 1982).

Burkman, A. (2012). Preparing novice teachers for success in elementary classrooms through professional development. *Delta Kappa Gamma Bulletin*, 78(3), 23–33.

Butt, G., & Lance, A. (2005). Secondary teacher workload and job satisfaction: do successful strategies for change exist?. *Educational Management Administration & Leadership*, 33(4), 401–422.

Callaghan, K. (2002). Nurturing the enthusiasm and ideals of new teachers through reflective practice. *Canadian Children*, 27(1), 38–41.

Cawte, K. (2020). Teacher crisis: critical events in the mid-career stage. *Australian Journal of Teacher Education (Online)*, 45(8), 75–92.

Gay, L.R., & Airasian, P. (2000). *Student Guide to Accompany Educational Research: Competencies for Analysis and Application*. New York: Merill.

Chaplain, R. P. (2008). Stress and psychological distress among trainee secondary teachers in England. *Educational Psychology*, 28(2), 195–209.

Chen, J., & Day, C. (2015). Tensions and dilemmas for Chinese teachers in responding to system wide change. In Gu, Q. (Ed.). *The work and lives of teachers in China* (pp.1-12). New York, NY: Routledge.

Chow, A. W. (2016). Teacher learning communities: The landscape of subject leadership. *International Journal of Educational Management*, 30(2), 287–307.

Chuanyou, B. (2006). Policies for compulsory education disparity between urban and rural areas in China. *Frontiers of Education in China*, 1(1), 40–55.

Chui, M. M. (2016). Private supplementary tutoring: Motivations and effects: A review study. *Journal of Education and Practice*, 7(27), 195–198.

Cohen, L., Manion, L., & Morrison, K. (2000). Action research. *Research Methods in Education*, 5, 226–244.

Cohen, L., Manion, L., & Morrison, K. (2013). *Research Methods in Education*. London; New York: Routledge.

Colnerud, G. (1997). Ethical conflicts in teaching. *Teaching and Teacher Education*, 13(6), 627–635.

Creswell, J. W. (1994). *Research Design: Qualitative and Quantitative* Approaches. London: Sage Publications.

Crutcher, P. A., & Naseem, S. (2016). Cheerleading and cynicism of effective mentoring in current empirical research. *Educational Review*, 68(1), 40–55.

Darling-Hammond, L. (1994). *Professional Development Schools: Schools for Developing a Profession*. Teachers College Press, 1234 Amsterdam Ave., New York, NY 10027.

Davidson, K. V.. (2009). Teacher stress in rural middle schools: teachers' perceptions of three contributing factors. (Doctoral dissertation, Mississippi State University, Mississippi, United States). Retrieved from https://scholarsjunction.msstate.edu/cgi/viewcontent.cgi?article=5215&context=td

Day, C. (2002). *Developing Teachers: The Challenges of Lifelong Learning*. Bristol: Taylor and Francis. https://doi.org/10.4324/9780203021316.

Dello-Iacovo, B. (2009). Curriculum reform and 'quality education' in China: An overview. *International Journal of Educational Development*, 29(3), 241–249.

Denzin, N. K., & Lincoln, Y. S. (2000). The discipline and practice of qualitative research. *Handbook of Qualitative Research*, 2, 1–28.

Denzin, N. K., & Lincoln, Y. S. (2008). *Strategies of Qualitative Inquiry* (Vol. 2). Thousand Oaks, CA.: Sage.

Dinham, S., & Scott, C. (2000). *Teachers' Work and the Growing Influence of Societal Expectations and Pressures*. Paper presented at the Annual meeting of the American Educational Research Association (New Orleans, LA, April 24–28, 2000).

Donnelly, R., & Fitzmaurice, M. (2011). Towards productive reflective practice in microteaching. *Innovations in Education and Teaching International*, 48(3), 335–346.

Dumont, H., Istance, D., & Benavides, F. (2010). *The Nature of Learning: Using Research to Inspire Practice*. Paris: OECD.

Elbaz, F. (1983). Teacher Thinking. A Study of Practical Knowledge. *Croom Helm Curriculum Policy and Research Series*. Nichols Publishing Company, 155 West 72nd Street, New York, NY 10023.

Elbaz, F. (1988). Critical reflection on teaching: Insights from Freire. *Journal of Education for Teaching*, 14(2), 171–181.

Erdamar, G., & Demirel, H. (2014). Investigation of work-family, family-work conflict of the teachers. *Procedia-Social and Behavioral Sciences*, 116, 4919–4924.

Evans, L. (2002). What is teacher development?. *Oxford Review of Education*, 28(1), 123–137.

Fantilli, R. D., & McDougall, D. E. (2009). A study of novice teachers: Challenges and supports in the first years. *Teaching and Teacher Education*, 25(6), 814–825.

Feiman-Nemser, S. (2001). Helping novices learn to teach: Lessons from an exemplary support teacher. *Journal of Teacher Education*, 52(1), 17–30.

Fessler, R., & Christensen, J. C. (1992). Teacher development as a career-long process. In R. Fessler & J. Christensen (Eds.), *The Teacher Career Cycle: Understanding and Guiding the Professional Development Of Teachers* (pp. 21–44). Boston: Allyn and Bacon.

Flores, M. A. (2001). Person and context in becoming a new teacher. *Journal of Education for Teaching: International research and pedagogy*, 27(2), 135–148.

Flores, M. A. (2004). The impact of school culture and leadership on new teachers' learning in the workplace. *International Journal of Leadership in Education*, 7(4), 297–318.

Fordasz, H., & Leder, G. (2006). Work patterns and stressors of experienced and novice mathematics teachers. *Australian Mathematics Teacher*, 62(3), 36–40.

Friedman, I. A. (2006). Classroom management and teacher stress and burnout. In Evertson, C. M., and Weinstein, C. S. (Eds). *Handbook of Classroom Management: Research, Practice, and Contemporary Issues* (pp. 925–944). Mahwah, N.J.: Lawrence Erlbaum Associates.

Friedman, I. A., & Farber, B. A. (1992). Professional self-concept as a predictor of teacher burnout. *The Journal of Educational Research*, 86(1), 28–35.

Fuller, F. (1969). Concerns of teachers: A developmental conceptualization. *American Educational Research Journal*, 6(2), 207–226.

Fultz, D., & Gimbert, B. (2009). Effective principal leadership for beginning teachers' development. *International Journal of Educational Leadership Preparation*, 4(2), n2.

Fwu, B. J., & Wang, H. H. (2002). The social status of teachers in Taiwan. *Comparative Education*, 38(2), 211–224.

Gall, M. D., Borg, W. R., & Gall, J. P. (1996). *Educational Research: An Introduction*. White Plains, N.Y.: Longman Publishing.

Gall, J. P., Gall, M. D., & Borg, W. R. (1999). *Applying Educational Research: A Practical Guide*. New York: Longman Publishing Group.

Gall, M. D., Gall. J. P., & Borg, W. R. (2007). *Educational Research: An Introduction*, New York: Longman Publishing Group.

Gay, L.R., & Airasian, P. (2000). *Student Guide to Accompany Educational Research: Competencies for Analysis and Application*. New York: Merill.

Gay, L. R., Mills, G. E., & Airasian, P. W. (2011). *Educational Research: Competencies for Analysis and Applications*. Boston: Pearson.

Germain, M., & Scandura, T. A. (2005). Grade inflation and student individual differences as systematic bias in faculty evaluations. *Journal of Instructional Psychology*, 32(1), 58–67.

Geving, A. M. (2007). Identifying the types of student and teacher behaviours associated with teacher stress. *Teaching & Teacher Education*, 23(5), 624–640.

Glatthorn, A. A. (1995). Teacher Development. In Anderson, L. W., and Dunkin, M. J. (Eds). *International Encyclopedia of Teaching and Teacher Education*. Oxford: Pergamon .

Glatthorn, A. A., & Fox, L. E. (1996). *Quality Teaching through Professional Development. Principals Taking Action Series*. Corwin Press, Inc., 2455 Teller Road, Thousand Oaks, CA 91320-2218 (paperback: ISBN-0-8039-6273-8; hardcover: ISBN-0-8039-6274-6).

Goepel, J. (2012). Upholding public trust: An examination of teacher professionalism and the use of Teachers' Standards in England. *Teacher Development*, 16(4), 489–505.

Gordon, S. P. (2004). *Professional Development for School Improvement: Empowering Learning Communities*. Boston: Allyn & Bacon.

Gratch, A. (2000). Teacher voice, teacher education, teaching professionals. *The High School Journal*, 83(3), 43-54.

Gratch, A. (2001). The culture of teaching and beginning teacher development. *Teacher Education Quarterly*, 28(4), 121–136.

Grosvenor, I., & Rose, R. (2001). *Doing Research in Special Education: Ideas into Practice*. London: David Fulton Publishers.

Guo, L. (2013). New curriculum reform in China and its impact on teachers. *Comparative and International Education*, 41(2), 6.

Guskey, T. R. (1999). *Evaluating Professional Development*. Thousand Oaks, Calif.: Corwin Press.

Hadar, L., & Brody, D. (2010). From isolation to symphonic harmony: Building a professional development community among teacher educators. *Teaching and Teacher Education*, 26(8), 1641–1651.

Hadar, L. L., & Brody, D. L. (2013). The interaction between group processes and personal professional trajectories in a professional development community for teacher educators. *Journal of Teacher Education*, 64(2), 145–161.

Hang Xiaoyu, Peng Lijuan, & Xie Yunli. (2010). Research on the standard and management system of teaching staff establishment of primary and secondary school—analysis on the current relevant policies of the country and more than ten. *Research in Educational Development*, 2010(008). 15-19 [in Chinese]. DOI: CNKI:SUN:SHGJ.0.2010-08-006

Hargreaves, A., & Fullan, M. G. (1992). *Understanding Teacher Development*. 1234 Amsterdam Avenue, New York, NY: Teachers College Press.

Hargreaves, A. (1995). Development and desire: a postmodern perspective. In Guskey, T., & Huberman, M. (Eds.), *Professional Development in Education: New Paradigms and Practices*. New York: Teachers' College Press.

Hebert, E., & Worthy, T. (2001). Does the first year of teaching have to be a bad one? A case study of success. *Teaching and Teacher Education*, 17(8), 897–911.

Hill, H. C. (2009). Fixing teacher professional development. *Phi Delta Kappan*, 90(7), 470–476.

Hodkinson, P., & Hodkinson, H. (2004). The significance of individuals' dispositions in workplace learning: A case study of two teachers. *Journal of Education and Work*, 17(2), 167–182.

Holstein, J. A., & Gubrium, J. F. (1995). *The Active Interview* (Vol. 37). Thousand Oaks, Calif.: Sage.

Hongbiao, Y. (2013). Implementing the national curriculum reform in China: A review of the decade. *Frontiers of Education in China*, 8(3), 331–359.

Hoyle, E., & Megarry, J. (Eds.). (2012).. *World Yearbook of Education 1980: The Professional Development of Teachers*. New York: Routledge. ISBN:978-0-415-38605-0.

Huang, F. (2004). Curriculum reform in contemporary China: Seven goals and six strategies. *Journal of Curriculum Studies*, 36(1), 101–115.

Huberman, M. (1989). The professional life cycle of teachers. *The Teachers College Record*, 91(1), 31–57.

Huberman, A. M., Grounauer, M. M., Marti, J. T., & Neufeld, J. (1993). The lives of teachers. *Phi Delta Kappan*, 78(6), 450–453.

Hue, M., & Li, W. (2008). *Classroom Management. Creating a Positive Learning Environment*. Hong Kong: Hong Kong University Press; London: Eurospan [distributor].

Huling, L., & Resta, V. (2001). *Teacher Mentoring as Professional Development*. Washington, DC.: ERIC Digest.

Johnson, B., & Christensen, L. B. (2014). *Educational Research: Quantitative, Qualitative, and Mixed Approaches* (Fifth edition.). Thousand Oaks, California: SAGE.

Joshi, K. R. (2018). Critical incidents for teachers' professional development. *Journal of NELTA Surkhet*, 5, 82–88.

Kajs, L. T. (2002). Framework for designing a mentoring program for novice teachers. *Mentoring and Tutoring*, 10(1), 57–69.

Katz, L. G. (1972). Developmental stages of preschool teachers. *The Elementary School Journal*, 73(1), 50–54.

Kennedy, E., & Shiel, G. (2010). Raising literacy levels with collaborative on-site professional development in an urban disadvantaged school. *The Reading Teacher*, 63(5), 372–383.

Koocher, G. P., & Campbell, L. F. (2016). Professional Ethics in the United States. In J. C. Norcross, G. R. VandenBos, D. K. Freedheim, & L. F. Campbell (Eds.), *APA handbook of clinical psychology: Education and profession* (pp. 301–337). American Psychological Association. https://doi.org/10.1037/14774-020

Koul, L. (1997). *Methodology of Educational Research* (3rd rev. and enl. ed.). New Delhi: Vikas Publishing House.

Kravale-Pauliņa, M., & Oļehnoviča, E. (2015). Human securitability: A participatory action research study involving novice teachers and youngsters. *Journal of Teacher Education for Sustainability*, 17(2), 91–107.

Kugel, P. (1993). How professors develop as teachers. *Studies in Higher Education*, 18(3), 315–328.

Kumi-Yeboah, A., & James, W. (2012). Transformational teaching experience of a novice teacher a narrative of an award-winning teacher. *Adult Learning*, 23(4), 170–177.

Kwok, P. L. Y. (2010). Demand intensity, market parameters and policy responses towards demand and supply of private supplementary tutoring in China. *Asia Pacific Education Review*, 11(1), 49–58.

Kyriacou, C. (2007). *Essential Teaching Skills*. Cheltenham: Nelson Thornes.

Kyriacou, C., & Kunc, R. (2007). Beginning teachers' expectations of teaching. *Teaching and Teacher Education*, 23(8), 1246–1257.

Lee, H. J. (2005). Developing a professional development program model based on teachers' needs. *Professional Educator*, 27, 39–49.

Lieberman, A., & Miller, L. (Eds.). (2001). *Teachers Caught in the Action: Professional Development that Matters* (Vol. 31). New York: Teachers College Press.

Lindgren, U. (2005). Experiences of beginning teachers in a school-based mentoring program in Sweden. *Educational Studies*, 31(3), 251–263.

Lipowski, K., Jorde, D., Prenzel, M., & Seidel, T. (2011). Expert views on the implementation of teacher professional development in European countries. *Professional Development in Education*, 37(5), 685–700.

Little, J. W. (1993). Teachers' professional development in a climate of educational reform. *Educational Evaluation and Policy Analysis*, 15(2), 129–151.

Little, J. W. (2002). Locating learning in teachers' communities of practice: Opening up problems of analysis in records of everyday work. *Teaching and Teacher Education*, 18(8), 917–946.

Lodico, M. G., Spaulding, D. T., & Voegtle, K. H. (2010). *Methods in Educational Research: From Theory to Practice* (2nd ed.). San Francisco, CA: Jossey-Bass.

Loucks-Horsley, S., Stiles, K. E., Mundry, S., Love, N., & Hewson, P. W. (2009). *Designing Professional Development for Teachers of Science and Mathematics*. Thousand Oaks, Calif.: Corwin Press.

Lundeen, C. A. (2004). Teacher development: The struggle of beginning teachers in creating moral (caring) classroom environments. *Early Child Development & Care*, 174(6), 549–564.

Ma, X., & MacMillan, R. B. (1999). Influences of workplace conditions on teachers' job satisfaction. *The Journal of Educational Research*, 93(1), 39–47.

Makovec, D. (2018). The teacher's role and professional development. *International Journal of Cognitive Research in Science, Engineering and Education*, 6(2), 33.

Marton, A. M. (2006). The cultural politics of curricular reform in China: A case study of geographical education in Shanghai. *Journal of Contemporary China*, 15(47), 233–254.

Maynard, T., & Furlong, J. (1995). Learning to teach and models of mentoring. In Kerry, T., & Mayes, A. S. (Eds.), *Issues in Mentoring* (pp. 10–24). London: Routledge in association with the Open University

Menekse, M. (2015). Computer science teacher professional development in the United States: A review of studies published between 2004 and 2014. *Computer Science Education*, 25(4), 325–350.

Meng, X., & Zhang, J. (2001). The two-tier labor market in urban China: Occupational segregation and wage differentials between urban residents and rural migrants in Shanghai. *Journal of Comparative Economics, 29*(3), 485–504.

Ministry of Education. (2001). The outline of curriculum reform of basic education (trial). *Heilongjiang Education*, 2001(10), 1–3 [in Chinese].

Ministry of Education. (2002). Ministry of Education's suggestions on reform and development of teacher education during the period of "Tenth Five Year-Plan". *Dynamic of Basic Education Reform*, 2002(9), 10-15 [in Chinese].

Ministry of Education. (2002). *New Curriculum Standard*. Beijing: Beijing Normal University Publishing House, 6. [in Chinese]

Ministry of Education. (2003). *Theory and Practice of Teacher Professionalization*. Beijing: People's Education Press [in Chinese].

Ministry of Education. (2005). *2003–2007 Action Plan for Invigorating Education*. Beijing: People's Education Press [in Chinese].

Ministry of Education. (2010). National mid-term and long-term education reform and development program outline (2010& 2012). *Ningxia Education*, 357 (9), 6–20 [in Chinese].

Ministry of Education. (2011). Ministry of Education's suggestions on strengthening teachers' training in primary and middle schools. *Teacher Training in Primary and Secondary Schools*, 294(01), 3–5 [in Chinese].

Morris, M., Chrispeels, J., & Burke, P. (2003). The power of two: Linking external with internal teachers' professional development. *Phi Delta Kappan, 84*(10), 764.

Murray, A. (2010). Empowering teachers through professional development. In *English teaching forum* (Vol. 48, No. 1, pp. 2–11). US Department of State. Bureau of Educational and Cultural Affairs, Office of English Language Programs, SA-5, 2200 C Street NW 4th Floor, Washington, DC 20037.

Newby, P. (2010). *Research Methods for Education*. Harlow, England; New York: Pearson Education.

Noe, R. A., Noe, A. W., & Bachhuber, J. A. (1990). An investigation of the correlates of career motivation. *Journal of Vocational Behavior, 37*(3), 340–356.

Onafowora, L. L. (2005). Teacher efficacy issues in the practice of novice teachers. *Educational Research Quarterly, 28*(4), 34.

Öztürk, M. (2008). *Induction into Teaching: Adaptation Challenges of Novice Teachers* (Master's thesis, Middle East Technical University).

Paula, L., & Grīnfelde, A. (2018). The role of mentoring in professional socialization of novice teachers. *Problems of Education in the 21st Century, 76*(3), 364.

Perry, P. (2012). Professional development: The Inspectorate in England and Wales. In Hoyle, E., & Megarry, J. (Eds.), *World Yearbook of Education 1980: The Professional Development of Teachers* (143–148). New York: Routledge.

Poon, C. L., & Lim, S. S. (2014). Transiting into inquiry science practice: Tales from a primary school. *In Inquiry into the Singapore Science Classroom* (pp. 139–164). Singapore: Springer.

Potthoff, D. E., Fredrickson, S. A., Batenhorst, E. V., & Tracy, G. E. (2001). Learning about cohorts—A master's degree program for teachers. *Action in Teacher Education*, 23(2), 36–42.

Punch, K. F., & Oancea, A. (2014). *Introduction to Research Methods in Education*. (2nd edition. / Keith F. Punch, Alis E. Oancea.). Los Angeles: Sage.

Qian, H., & Walker, A. (2013). How principals promote and understand teacher development under curriculum reform in China. *Asia-Pacific Journal of Teacher Education*, 41(3), 304–315.

Qi-quan, Z. (2006). Curriculum reform in China: Challenges and reflections. *Frontiers of Education in China*, 1(3), 370–382.

Richards, J. C., & Lockhart, C. (1994). *Reflective Teaching in Second Language Classrooms*. Cambridge, England: Cambridge University Press.

Ritchie, J., Lewis, J., Nicholls, C. M., & Ormston, R. (Eds.). (2013). *Qualitative Research Practice: A Guide for Social Science Students and Researchers*. London; CA.; New Delhi; Singapore: SAGE.

Saldaña, J. (2015). *The Coding Manual for Qualitative Researchers*. Thousand Oaks, CA.: SAGE.

Sales, A., Traver, J. A., & García, R. (2011). Action research as a school-based strategy in intercultural professional development for teachers. *Teaching and Teacher Education*, 27(5), 911–919.

Salleh, H., & Tan, C. (2013). Novice Teachers Learning from Others: Mentoring in Shanghai Schools. *Australian Journal of Teacher Education*, 38(3). 152-165.

Sargent, T., & Hannum, E. (2005). Keeping teachers happy: Job satisfaction among primary school teachers in rural Northwest China. *Comparative Education Review*, 49(2), 173–204.

Sergiovanni, T. J. (1998). Leadership as pedagogy, capital development and school effectiveness. *International Journal of Leadership in Education Theory and Practice*, 1(1), 37–46.

Servage, L. (2009). Who is the "professional" in a professional learning community? An exploration of teacher professionalism in collaborative professional development settings. *Canadian Journal of Education/Revue canadienne de l'éducation*, 32(1), 149–171.

Shan, D. (2002). Curriculum reform promotes quality education. *China Education Newspaper* [in Chinese].

Shawer, S. (2010). Classroom-level teacher professional development and satisfaction: Teachers learn in the context of classroom-level curriculum development. *Professional Development in Education*, 36(4), 597–620.

Shulman, L. S. (1997). Disciplines of inquiry in education: A new overview. In Jaeger, R. M. (Ed.), *Complementary Methods for Research in Education* (2nd ed., pp. 3–39). Washington, D.C.: American Educational Research Association.

Smalley, S. W., & Smith, A. R. (2017). Professional development needs of mid-career agriculture teachers. *Journal of Agricultural Education*, 58(4), 282–290.

Smith, C. J. (2002). *Teacher Professional Development: Exploring Organizational Contexts Across Secondary School Types*. Unpublished doctoral dissertation. College of Education, Ashland University.

State Council. (2012). State Council's suggestions on strengthening the construction of teaching team. *Gazette of People's Government of Hainan Province* (18), 8–12 [in Chinese].

Steffy, B. E. (2000). *Life Cycle of the Career Teacher*. Thousand Oaks, Calif.: Kappa Delta Pi; Corwin Press.

Strati, A. D., Schmidt, J. A., & Maier, K. S. (2017). Perceived challenge, teacher support, and teacher obstruction as predictors of student engagement. *Journal of Educational Psychology*, 109(1), 131–147. doi:10.1037/edu0000108

Suter, W. N. (2012). *Introduction to Educational Research: A Critical Thinking Approach*. Thousand Oaks, Calif.: Sage Publications, Inc.

Tang, S. Y. F., & Choi, P. L. (2004). The development of personal, intercultural and professional competence in international field experience in initial teacher education. *Asia Pacific Education Review*, 5, 50-63.

Tang, S. Y., Wong, A. K., & Cheng, M. M. (2016). Examining professional learning and the preparation of professionally competent teachers in initial teacher education. *Teachers and Teaching*, 22(1), 54–69.

Tao, W. (2012). The ten years of the basic education curriculum reform experimental teaching in Beijing: progress and issues in subject teaching. *Educational Science Research*, 208(07), 5-17 [in Chinese].

Travers, C. J., & Cooper, C. L. (1996). *Teachers Under Pressure: Stress in the Teaching Profession*. London: Routledge.

Tu, Y., LI, W. (2005). An investigation report on the employment situations of the normal university graduates. *Education & Economy*, 2005(3), 4-6 [in Chinese]. DOI: 10.3969/j.issn.1003-4870.2005.03.002

United Nations Educational, Scientific and Cultural Organization (UNESCO). (2012). *Youth and Skills: Putting Education to Work*. UNESCO: Paris, France.

Valenčič Zuljan, M., & Marentič Požarnik, B. (2014). Induction and Early-career Support of Teachers in Europe. *European Journal of Education*, 49(2), 192–205.

Van Driel, J. H., Beijaard, D., & Verloop, N. (2001). Professional development and reform in science education: The role of teachers' practical knowledge. *Journal of Research in Science Teaching*, 38(2), 137–158.

Villegas-Reimers, E. (2003). *Teacher Professional Development: An International Review of the Literature*. Paris: International Institute for Educational Planning.

Vonk, J. H. C. (1995). *Conceptualizing Novice Teachers' Professional Development: A Base for Supervisory Interventions*. Paper presented at the Annual Meeting of the American Educational Research Association (San Francisco, CA, April18-2,1995).

Wallen, N. E., & Fraenkel, J. R. (2001). *Educational Research: A Guide to the Process* (2nd ed.). *Mahwah, N.J.; London:* Lawrence Erlbaum Associates.

Walliman, N. (2010). *Research Methods: The Basics*. Abingdon: Routledge.

Wang, H. H. (2016). Dangling between the traditional and the reformist: Reality shocks for student teachers amid the tide of educational reform in a test-oriented culture. In *Chinese Education Models in a Global Age* (pp. 149–162). Springer: Singapore.

Weasmer, J., Woods, A. M., & Coburn, T. (2008). Enthusiastic and growing teachers: Individual dispositions, critical incidences, and family supports. *Education*, 129(1), 21-35.

Whitaker, S. D. (2000). What do first-year special education teachers need? Implications for induction programs. *Teaching Exceptional Children*, 33(1), 28–36.

Wiersma, W., & Jurs, S. G. (2009). *Research Methods in Education: An Introduction*. Boston, Mass.: Pearson/Allyn and Bacon.

Winter, J. S. (2011). Sustaining teacher educators: Finding professional renewal through vocation and avocation. *SRATE Journal*, 20(1), 27–32.

Hawkins, J. (2015). *Student Engagement: Leadership Practices, Perspectives and Impact of Technology* (J. Hawkins, Ed.). New York: Nova Publishers.

Wubbels, T. (2011). An international perspective on classroom management: What should prospective teachers learn?. *Teaching Education*, 22(2), 113–131.

Xu, M. Y. (2013). Investigation on the Current situation and influencing factors of new teachers' professional development (Master's thesis, East China Normal University, Shanghai, China). Retrieved from http://big5.oversea.cnki.net/kcms/download.aspx?filename=htry jmnvjtxu0npledkzxuqzgzavxvjvhrkjwbf5mqwt0u5kncs9uzruzkspwss10uwg1aqxmq3fvw= 0tu10wb3kgvwrxawb3bejenp5gvnz2ldlxtwnxvmtgvez1t0ywabndephlzkvfzhf3r1onvn92 umj&dflag=pdfdown&tablename=cmfd201402

Zeichner, K. M., & Tabachnick, B. R. (1985). The development of teacher perspectives: Social strategies and institutional control in the socialization of beginning teachers. *Journal of Education for Teaching*, 11(1), 1–25.

Zhang, X., & Kanbur, R. (2005). Spatial inequality in education and health care in China. *China Economic Review*, 16(2), 189–204.

Zhou, J. (2014). Teacher education changes in China: 1974–2014. *Journal of Education for Teaching*, 40(5), 507–523.

Zhu, H. (2010). Curriculum reform and professional development: A case study on Chinese teacher educators. *Professional Development in Education*, 36(1–2), 373–391.

PETER LANG
PROMPT

Peter Lang Prompts offer our authors the opportunity to publish original research in small volumes that are shorter and more affordable than traditional academic monographs. With a faster production time, this concise model gives scholars the chance to publish time-sensitive research, open a forum for debate, and make an impact more quickly. Like all Peter Lang publications, Prompts are thoroughly peer reviewed and can even be included in series.

For further information, please contact:

editorial@peterlang.com

To order, please contact our Customer Service Department:

peterlang@presswarehouse.com (within the U.S.)
orders@peterlang.com (outside the U.S.)

Visit our website: www.peterlang.com

Prompts include:

Claudia Aburto Guzmán, *Poesía reciente de voces en diálogo con la ascendencia hispano-hablante en los Estados Unidos: Antología breve*. ISBN 978-1-4331-5207-8. 2020

William Robert Adamson, *Mine Own Familiar Friend: The Relationship between Gerard Hopkins and Robert Bridges*. ISBN 978-1-80079-485-6. 2021

Tywan Ajani, *Barriers to Rebuilding the African American Community: Understanding the Issues Facing Today's African Americans from a Social Work Perspective*. ISBN 978-1-4331-7681-4. 2020

Macarena Areco, *Bolaño Constelaciones: Literatura, sujetos, territorios*. ISBN 978-1-4331-7575-6. 2020

Robin Burgess (ed.), *FRANCESCO ALGAROTTI: AN ESSAY ON THE OPERA (Saggio sopra l'opera in musica) The editions of 1755 and 1763*. ISBN 978-1-80079-505-1. 2022

Desrine Bogle. *The Transatlantic Culture Trade: Caribbean Creole Proverbs from Africa, Europe, and the Caribbean*. ISBN 978-1-4331-5723-3. 2020

Jean-François Caron. *Irresponsible Citizenship: The Cultural Roots of the Crisis of Authority in Times of Pandemic*. ISBN 978-1-4331-8908-1. 2021

Jean-François Caron, *The Great Lockdown: Western Societies and the Fear of Death*. ISBN 978-1-4331-9535-8. 2022

Marcílio de Freitas and Marilene Corrêa da Silva Freitas, *The Future of Amazonia in Brazil: A Worldwide Tragedy*. ISBN 978-1-4331-7793-4. 2020

Mihai Dragnea. *Christian Identity Formation Across the Elbe in the Tenth and Eleventh Centuries.* Christianity and Conversion in Scandinavia and the Baltic Region, c. 800–1600, vol. 1. ISBN 978-1-4331-8431-4. 2021

Janet Farrell Leontiou, *The Doctor Still Knows Best: How Medical Culture Is Still Marked by Paternalism.* Health Communication, vol. 15. ISBN 978-1-4331-7322-6. 2020

Clare Gorman (ed.), *Miss-representation: Women, Literature, Sex and Culture.* ISBN 978-1-78874-586-4. 2020

Eva Marín Hlynsdóttir. *Gender in Organizations: The Icelandic Female Council Manager.* ISBN 978-1-4331-7729-3. 2020

Micol Kates, *Towards a Vegan-Based Ethic: Dismantling Neo-Colonial Hierarchy Through an Ethic of Lovingkindness.* ISBN 978-1-4331-7797-2. 2020

Sunho Kim, *Inner Mongolia, Outer Mongolia: The History of the Division of the "Descendants of Chinggis Khan" in the 20th Century.* ISBN 978-1-4331-8185-6. 2022

Feridoon Koohi-Kamali (ed.), *Exploring Roots of Inequality in Latin America and Peru.* ISBN 978-1-4331-8989-0. 2021

Guy Merchant, Cathy Burnett, Jeannie Bulman, and Emma Rogers. *Stacking Stories: Exploring the Hinterland of Education.* ISBN 978-1-80079-686-7. 2022

Matt Qvortrup, *Winners and Losers: Which Countries are Successful and Why?.* ISBN 978-1-80079-405-4. 2021

Peter Raina, *Doris Lessing – A Life Behind the Scenes: The Files of the British Intelligence Service MI5.* ISBN 978-1-80079-183-1. 2021

Peter Raina (trans.), *Heinrich von Kleist Poems.* ISBN 978-1-80079-043-8. 2020

Josiane Ranguin, *Mediating the Windrush Children: Caryl Phillips and Horace Ové.* ISBN 978-1-4331-7424-7. 2020

Dylan Scudder, *Coffee and Conflict in Colombia: Part of the Pentalemma Series on Managing Global Dilemmas.* ISBN 978-1-4331-7568-8. 2020

Dylan Scudder, *Conflict Minerals in the Democratic Republic of Congo: Part of the Pentalemma Series on Managing Global Dilemmas.* ISBN 978-1-4331-7561-9. 2020

Dylan Scudder, *Mining Conflict in the Philippines: Part of the Pentalemma Series on Managing Global Dilemmas.* ISBN 978-1-4331-7632-6. 2020

Dylan Scudder, *Multi-Hazard Disaster in Japan: Part of the Pentalemma Series on Managing Global Dilemmas.* ISBN 978-1-4331-7530-5. 2020

Wesley A. Stroud, *Education for Liberation, Education for Dignity: The Story of St. Monica's School of Basic Learning for Women.* ISBN 978-1-4331-7911-2. 2021

Geanneti Tavares Salomon, *Fashion and Irony in «Dom Casmurro».* ISBN 978-1-78997-972-5. 2021

Zia Ul Haque Shamsi, *South Asia Needs Hybrid Peace.* ISBN 978-1-4331-9422-1. 2022

Mohammad Rafiqul Islam Talukdar, *Local Government Budgetary Autonomy: Evidence from Bangladesh*. ISBN 978-1-80079-528-0. 2022

Shai Tubali, *Cosmos and Camus: Science Fiction Film and the Absurd*. ISBN 978-1-78997-664-9. 2020

Angela Williams, *Hip Hop Harem: Women, Rap and Representation in the Middle East*. ISBN 978-1-4331-7295-3. 2020

Ivan Zhavoronkov (trans.), *The Socio-Cultural and Philosophical Origins of Science* by Anatoly Nazirov. ISBN 978-1-4331-7228-1. 2020

www.ingramcontent.com/pod-product-compliance
Ingram Content Group UK Ltd.
Pitfield, Milton Keynes, MK11 3LW, UK
UKHW021828210426
5322IPUK00003B/68